Sorting Out the Chaos for Public Relations Leaders

Marc Compte-Pujol /
Joan Cuenca-Fontbona /
Paula Pineda-Martínez (eds.)

Sorting Out the Chaos for Public Relations Leaders

PETER LANG

Berlin - Bruxelles - Chennai - Lausanne - New York - Oxford

Library of Congress Cataloging-in-Publication
A CIP catalog record for this book has been applied for at the Library of Congress.

Bibliographic information published by the Deutsche Nationalbibliothek
The Deutsche Nationalbibliothek lists this publication in the Deutsche Nationalbibliografie; detailed bibliographic data is available on the Internet at http://dnb.d-nb.de.

ISBN 978-3-631-90776-4 (Print)
E-ISBN 978-3-631-92404-4 (E-PDF)
E-ISBN 978-3-631-92405-1 (E-PUB)
DOI.10.3726/b22162

Published by Peter Lang GmbH, Berlin, Germany

info@peterlang.com - www.peterlang.com

Preface

In this preface, I have the privilege of introducing a group of Portuguese, Spanish, and Latin American scholars' timely edited publication, "Sorting out the chaos for public relations leaders." As a long-time colleague of this distinguished group of academics and a member of the boards of several U.S.-based and international organizations dedicated to the advancement of public relations research and practice, I was immediately drawn into the compelling set of topics the authors have documented, especially on countries and regions underrepresented in the public relations body of knowledge. The authors, who are experts in their respective fields, offer insights and analyses based on empirical research and theoretical frameworks, using a variety of methods, such as discourse and content analyses, quantitative surveys and qualitative interviews, and comprehensive literature reviews.

This edited volume has been coordinated by Marc Compte-Pujol, a full-time lecturer of advertising, communication, and public relations at Universitat Oberta de Catalunya and a part-time lecturer at Blanquerna—Ramon Llull University in Barcelona, Spain; Joan Cuenca-Fontbona, Tenured professor of strategic communication and public relations at Blanquerna; and Paula Pineda-Martínez, assistant professor of strategic communication and public relations at the University of the Basque Country.

From the first chapter on, readers will learn about the complexity of the study and practice of public relations in an increasingly conflict-ridden world, and the demanding responsibilities of leaders to manage communications and the reputational and relational challenges in times when audiences are greatly segmented, the media environment is fragmented, and the geopolitical, economic, and social landscapes are in flux. A time when public relations professionals need to become trusted advisers to top management and social listeners to capture the dynamic nature of issues, contexts, and stakeholders.

Throughout these chapters, a clear picture of the disruptive changes that have become the new normal for organizations and society is explained and supported by primary data, relevant citations, cases, and illustrations. These changes include armed conflicts in several latitudes, extreme climate events, and large economic gaps among segments of the population that produce poverty and inequality with the potential for violence, among other phenomena with unpredictable consequences for organizations and their stakeholders.

The strategic and socially oriented public relations function can help organizations face today's challenges with an emphasis on organizational agility, ethics, and responsibility. Research-based and audience-oriented public relations practices reduce ambiguity and uncertainty, providing actionable insights to organizational leaders for clever and prompt decision-making and responses. As the authors indicate, public relations is a modern profession that evolves in dynamic environments plagued with chaos. This volume presents the latest research in this area of study with an emphasis on strategy and value generation in disruptive global and regional contexts.

In conclusion, this edited book aims to contribute to the advancement of knowledge and practice of public relations, and it provides useful references and guidance for students, researchers, and professionals.

Juan-Carlos Molleda, PhD
Edwin L. Artzt Dean and Professor
School of Journalism and Communication, University of Oregon

Contents

Part Three Local Contexts and Global Trends in Public Relations

Marc Compte-Pujol, Joan Cuenca-Fontbona, and Paula Pineda-Martínez

Introduction

The volume you have in your hands includes a series of works derived from various scientific research that focus on the leadership of people responsible for public relations and communication in organizations. These leaders face constant and sudden changes in their environment, to which any organization is exposed. Unfortunately, this context has become normalized.

The starting point is found in the fundamental purpose of public relations, a discipline dedicated to managing communication in environments characterized by instability, insecurity and complexity. This may include dynamic, uncertain or conflictive scenarios, as well as embarrassing crises and information overload among various social actors. Since its inception, public relations have conceived and executed communication strategies aimed at mitigating conflicts that may affect the reputation of the parties involved, while promoting authentic and solid relationships between the organizations they have represented and their various publics, as well as with other social groups they have been able to serve. This discipline, based on empirical research, has developed strategies, facilitated decision-making and trained the different actors involved to face turbulent environments with proven effectiveness (Anderson-Meli & Koshy, 2020; Cutlip & Center, 1978; Grunig & Hunt, 2000; Heide & Simonsson, 2015; Johansen et al., 2012; Kim et al., 2019; Kunsch, 1986; L'Etang, 2009; L'Etang et al., 2016; López Menacho, 2018; Losada-Díaz, 2018; Matilla & Marca, 2013; Mazzei & Butera, 2021; Murphy, 2000; Ulmer et al., 2018; Wilcox et al., 2015; Xifra, 2017; Yaxley, 2022).

The hyperconnected society we live in is a constant melting pot of chaos and permacrisis (Sriramesh et al., 2020; Taylor, 2010). The speed with which information about any event or situation spreads raises all the alarms and shapes the communicative and relational interactions between social actors, both at local and supranational levels. In this context, the ability to reach agreements among disagreements becomes more crucial than ever.

Non-linear and disruptive change has become the norm for organizations and society in general (Ragas & Ragas, 2021). War conflicts, climate change, drought, poverty, inequality and the silent increase in violence, abuse and exploitation are just some of the most notable events today, with economic, political, technological, and social consequences whose scope remains unpredictable for organizations and their audiences.

In this context, called with the acronym VUCA (Volatile, Uncertain, Complex and Ambiguous) (Baran & Woznyj, 2021; Dühring & Zerfass, 2021; Ragas & Ragas, 2021), public relations emerge as a vital resource to help organizations to address these challenges. This is because the strategic component of communication, inherent to the discipline, is essential to confer agility to the organization (Baran & Woznyj, 2021; Dühring & Zerfass, 2021; Ragas & Ragas, 2021; Werder, 2021). In this sense, the praxis of public relations plays a fundamental role in reducing uncertainty and ambiguity, simplifies the complex issues facing the organization and monitors any volatile factors that could otherwise increase organizational fragility and complicate its understanding for key audiences. The corrective that public relations provide is to persistently build positive images and cultivate support and alliances with these audiences (Dühring & Zerfass, 2021). Furthermore, by providing constant interaction with stakeholders, public relations fosters innovation and facilitates organizational evolution (Ragas & Ragas, 2021), with two-way communication being the cornerstone of this adaptation process (Baran & Woznyj, 2021).

Recovering the notion of agility, understood as the ability of individuals, teams or organizations to anticipate and respond quickly to change (Baran & Woznyj, 2021), this competence becomes essential among leaders in charge of guiding their organizations in the midst of turbulence (Baran & Woznyj, 2021; Dühring & Zerfass, 2021; Ragas & Ragas, 2021). According to Baran and Woznyj (2021, p. 1), "For organizations, agility involves ongoing sensing and monitoring of the environment and of the organization's stakeholders to detect and respond rapidly to weak signals of threats or opportunities." Therefore, it is not surprising that authors such as Dühring and Zerfass (2021, p. 96) highlight that public relations, based on theories such as systems theory (Cutlip & Center,1978; Grunig & Hunt, 2000), the theory of complexity (Gilpin & Murphy, 2008; Murphy, 1996, 2000; Nothhaft & Wehmeier, 2007) and contingency theory (Long & Hazelton, 1987), address aspects related to the agility that should characterize the professional profile of public relations and, consequently, enable to manage the tumultuous environments that disrupt organizations. Thus, whether due to increased confusion, noise, or lack of understanding of the organizational environment, each of these phenomena represents a struggle and an opportunity that continually tests the practice of public relations (or demands responses by part of public relations).

Effective leadership that speeds up the handling of these scenarios requires a detailed analysis of the context, a crucial aspect to promote precise and appropriate strategies. According to authors such as Baran, Woznyj, Dühring and Zerfass, public relations leadership, through the communication strategy it promotes in organizations, must necessarily consider both the internal and external environment, which includes a variety of publics, such as employees, government authorities, industrial actors, competitors, activists, clients, among other audiences.

This work encapsulates the essence of public relations as a discipline that confronts everyday chaos and uncertainty. Compiled from the dissertations, concerns, and reflections of 25 scholars from diverse cultures and perspectives in the field of public relations, this book offers the reader a series of advanced research that explores the fundamental role of public relations in generating value for organizations in such an intelligible global context.

The first part of the book, titled "Powerful Public Relations Skills," offers a detailed analysis of how public relations tools can strengthen the communication management of organizations in critical situations when applied strategically. In the first chapter, Bianca Persici Toniolo and Hugo Sampaio, from the Beira Interior University, highlight the importance of the spokesperson and the development of communication strategies in the context of a crisis. Through a case study, which empirically examines the fundamental aspects of media training in an environmental crisis, the authors provide research with a specific objective: to evaluate which spokesperson profile prevails in their communication during a crisis when the member of the Government has a double competence, both in terms of technical expertise and political authority.

According to the European Communication Monitor 2023 report (Zerfass et al., 2023), leadership emerges as one of the thematic areas that will shape the future of strategic communication. Research in this area enables an expansion of reflections and debates on its relevance and daily application in the communication of organizations, especially in the chaotic context that characterizes current normality. In this context, Alejandro Álvarez-Nobell, Gabriel Sadi and María Belén Barroso contribute significantly by addressing a trending topic in public relations: the evaluation of the role of empathy in the leadership of internal communication and its impact on the work environment of public relations professionals in 20 Latin American countries. Starting from the question: "What happens with public relations in a society marked by risk, uncertainty, insecurity and economic, social and environmental crisis?" the authors debate how empathy in the leadership of internal public relations generates changes in the way in which organizations communicate with their various internal audiences, and how this positively impacts their efficiency in a context of turbulence.

One of the most significant challenges that public institutions face today is the construction of relationships of trust in an environment characterized by misinformation, where fake news, hoaxes and other content that circulates digitally abounds (Almansa-Martínez & Fernández-Souto, 2020; Zerfass et al., 2023; Casero-Ripollés, 2018; Rodríguez-Fernández, 2019; Vargo et al., 2017). In this context, these organizations need to communicate their purpose, address the issues that concern society and, in this way, maintain their institutional legitimacy. The second part of the book, titled "Institutional Communication and Institutional Relations," seeks to enrich the debate on this topic from different approaches. In the third chapter, "A public relations perspective on communication challenges in public institutions," researchers Joan Cuenca-Fontbona, Marc Compte-Pujol, Mariana Sueldo and Ramon Martin-Guart explore the practice of communication service in municipalities with populations between 10,000 and 20,000 inhabitants in the province of Barcelona (Spain). Their contribution examines how these institutions communicate with their residents with the aim of improving transparency, public access to information and good governance. The study concludes that, although municipal communication departments widely use digital communication, they underestimate its particularities as a space for participation and dialogue between political representatives and citizens. Consequently, these institutions are not yet moving toward a specialized strategic direction in public relations that is aligned with a context of participatory democracy and new public governance.

Another example that highlights the importance of public relations in the effectiveness of institutional communication in public administration is the one presented by the professors at the University of Vic-Central University of Catalonia, Mariola Tàrrega Moltó, Jordi de San Eugenio Vela and Xavier Ginesta Portet. Their research focuses on demonstrating the fundamental role of public relations in establishing and maintaining relationships of trust and mutual commitment between the various actors involved in territorial branding projects, with the aim of turning citizens into brand ambassadors.

The regulation of lobbies is one of the pending issues in Spain. The chapter that closes the second part of the book, "Lobbies and pressure groups: Analyzing revolving doors in Spain's public relations," presents research that undoubtedly contributes to the important normative framework of the practice of institutional communication. Professors Antonio Castillo-Esparcia, Elizabet Castillero-Ostio and Andrea Moreno-Cabanillas from the University of Malaga examine Spanish cases of "revolving doors," understood as "the practice whereby people who have held political or government positions move on to work as professional lobbyists or in private companies, and vice versa." The research reveals relevant connections between the elites of political-institutional power and economic-business power in Spain during the last five decades, which represents a threat to the legitimacy of the public function and undermines society's trust in institutions.

The added value of public relations lies in training based on critical thinking, creativity, research, and innovative skills applied to various institutional, corporate, or business settings. The third and final part of the book, titled "Local Contexts and Global Trends in Public Relations," seeks to offer a prospective vision of the direction that the practice of public relations is taking, with the aim of increasing value for organizations in the new global normality, characterized by its chaotic complexity. Therefore, in the sixth chapter, researchers Ana Belén Fernández-Souto, Montse Vázquez Gestal and Iván Puentes-Rivera, from the University of Vigo, examine the evolution of business communication clusters in Spain to understand the progress and challenges that faces a profession that seeks to contribute to organizations being able to anticipate and address changes in their environment. Their work, "Analysis of the communication structures of Spanish clusters in Spain (2017–2022)," focuses on the study of the available resources, the most common communication practices, and the level of professionalization in these environments. Their revealing findings show that the professionalization of the departments of the clusters studied continues to be an area for improvement in Spain, since organizations do not consider it a priority to establish an internal structure for the management of communication and reputation in the face of a constantly changing environment.

From a local perspective, the seventh chapter is titled "The situation of strategic communication and public relations in the Dominican Republic" and has co-authors Onoris Metz-Galán, Adrián Cordero-Redondo, Alejandro Álvarez-Nobell and Ana Bélgica Guichardo-Bretón. This research aims to understand the reality of the professional communication sector in the Dominican Republic in the current context of change. The authors point out the great potential of the field of communication in outsourced services. However, they also highlight that the sector in general is in an embryonic stage, marked by ethical dilemmas.

The last contribution, entitled "The evolution of public relations trends over the last five years according to the most relevant professional reports in the sector," closes the prospective panorama of the sector. To identify the trends that have emerged during the pandemic, academics María Isabel Míguez González, Juan Manuel Corbacho Valencia and Jesús Pérez Seoane from the University of Vigo review the most notable annual reports of professional associations both at the Spanish and international level (such as DIRCOM, EUPRERA, USC Center for Public Relations and Corporate Excellence Center for Reputation Leadership). The authors explain that the COVID-19 health crisis has served to strengthen and consolidate the essential trends that were observed in the years prior to the pandemic, such as ethics, purpose, sustainability, the spread of fake news and post-truth, the need to generate trust, leadership, and transparency, many of which are addressed in the studies that make up this work. Furthermore, they point out that where the pandemic has caused significant alterations is in the communication industry in terms of digitalization and the use of various channels and platforms.

This presentation has not attempted to immerse itself in the debate on the increasingly chaotic global context in which society is immersed, nor to discuss the foundations of public relations that address, on this occasion, certain constructs such as agility, a form that is defined by rapid adaptation to change. Its purpose has been to introduce the different contributions from the various approaches that focus on providing information, reflections and proposals to help organizations understand and evolve (and for professionals in the communication sector to broaden their perspectives) in the face of the current reality, characterized by its volatility, uncertainty, complexity and ambiguity or, as it is already public, by its fragility, non-linearity, anxiety and incomprehension, through very thoughtful and thus strategic communication with organizational publics, which constitutes the essence of Public Relations.

References

Almansa-Martínez, A., & Fernández-Souto, A.-B. (2020). Professional Public Relations (PR) trends and challenges. *El profesional de la información, 29*(3).

Anderson-Meli, L., & Koshy, S. (2020). *Public relations crisis communication: A new model.* Taylor & Francis.

Baran, B. E., & Woznyj, H. M. (2021). Managing VUCA: The human dynamics of agility. *Organizational Dynamics, 50*(2).

Casero-Ripollés, A. (2018). Research on political information and social media: Key points and challenges for the future. *El profesional de la información, 27*(5), 964–974.

Cutlip, S., & Center, A. H. (1978). *Effective public relations* (5th ed.). Prentice Hall.

Dühring, L., & Zerfass, A. (2021). The Triple Role of Communications in Agile Organizations. *International Journal of Strategic Communication*, 15(2), 93–112.

Gilpin, D., & Murphy, P. (2008). *Crisis management in a complex world.* Oxford Scholarship Online.

Grunig, J. E., & Hunt, T. (2000). *Dirección de Relaciones Públicas.* Gestión.

Heide, M., & Simonsson, C. (2015). Struggling with internal crisis communication: A balancing act between paradoxical tensions. *Public Relations Inquiry, 4*(2), 223–255.

Johansen, W., Aggerholm, H. K., & Frandsen, F. (2012) Entering new territory: A study of internal crisis management and crisis communication in organizations. *Public Relations Review, 38*(2), 270–279.

Kim, Y., Kang, M., Lee, E., & Yang, S.-U. (2019). Exploring crisis communication in the internal context of an organization: Examining moderated and mediated effects of employee-organization relationships on crisis outcomes. *Public Relations Review, 45*(3), 101777.

Kunsch, M. M. K. (1986). *Planejamento de Relações Públicas na Comunicação Integrada* (3rd ed.). Summus Editorial.

L'Etang, J. (2009). *Relaciones públicas: Conceptos, práctica y crítica*. UOC.

L'Etang, J., Mckie, D., Snow, N., & Xifra, J. (2016). *The Routledge handbook of critical public relations*. Routledge.

Long, L. V., & Hazelton, V. (1987). Public relations: A theoretical and practical response. *Public Relations Review, 13*(2), 3–13.

López Menacho, J. (2018). *SOS. 25 casos para superar una crisis de reputación digital*. UOC.

Losada-Díaz, J. C. (2018). *(NO)CRISIS. La comunicación de crisis en un mundo conectado*. UOC.

Matilla, K., & Marca, G. (2013). Issues management as a mediated activity in a changing media sphere. In E. Comas, J. Cuenca, & K. Zilles (Eds.), *Life without media* (pp. 223–247). Peter Lang.

Mazzei, A., & Butera, A. (2021). Internal crisis communication. In L. R. Men & A. Tkalac (Eds.), *Current trends and issues in internal communication: Theory and practice* (pp. 165–181). Palgrave Macmillan.

Murphy, P. (1996). Chaos theory as a model for managing issues and crises. *Public Relations Review, 22*(2), 95–113.

Murphy, P. (2000). Symmetry, contingency, complexity: Accommodating uncertainty in public relations theory. *Public Relations Review, 26*(4), 447–462.

Nothhaft, H., & Wehmeier, S. (2007). Coping with Complexity: Sociocybernetics as a Framework for Communication Management. *International Journal of Strategic Communication*, 1(3), 151–168.

Ragas, M., & Ragas, T. (2021) Understanding agile for strategic communicators: Foundations, implementations, and implications. *International Journal of Strategic Communication, 15*(2), 80–92.

Rodríguez-Fernández, L. (2019). Desinformación: retos profesionales para el sector de la comunicación. *El profesional de la información*, *28*(3).

Sriramesh, K., Tkalac Verčič, A., & Vercic, D. (2020). A world in crisis: The role of public relations. *Corporate Communications: An International Journal*, *25*(1), 1–2.

Taylor, M. (2010). Toward a holistic organizational approach to understanding crisis. In W. T. Coombs & S. J. Holladay (Eds.), *The handbook of crisis communication*. Blackwell.

Ulmer, R. R., Sellnow, T. L., & Seeger, M. W. (2018). *Effective crisis communication: Moving from crisis to opportunity*. Sage.

Vargo, C. J., Guo, L., & Amazeen, M. A. (2017). The agenda-setting power of fake news: A big data analysis of the online media landscape from 2014 to 2016. *New Media & Society*, *20*(5), 2028–2049.

Werder, K. P. (2021). Editor's Introduction. *International Journal of Strategic Communication*, *15*(2), 77-7.

Wilcox, D. L., Cameron, G. T., & Reber, B. H. (2015). *Public relations. Strategies and tactics* (Global ed.). Pearson Education.

Xifra, J. (2017). *Manual de Relaciones Públicas e Institucionales* (3rd ed.). Tecnos.

Yaxley, H. (2022). Gestión de riesgos, problemas y comunicación de crisis: desarrollar una práctica profesional sostenible en Alison Theaker. In *El Manual de Comunicación y Relaciones Públicas*. Profit.

Zerfass, A., Tench, R., Verčič, D., Moreno, A., Buhmann, A., & Hagelstein, J. (2023). *European Communication Monitor 2023. Looking back and ahead: 15 years of research on strategic communication*. EUPRERA/EACD.

Part One Powerful Public Relations Skills

Bianca Persici Toniolo, and Hugo Sampaio

From technical specialist to government authority: Media training in risk and crisis communication

Abstract: In this chapter, we assessed the discourse of the Portuguese Civil Protection spokesperson, Patrícia Gaspar, during events of risk and crisis triggered by natural disasters of meteorological phenomena. We used the qualitative method of discourse analysis to verify whether the voice of the technical expert or that of the political authority prevails in her communication. We also discussed verbal and nonverbal aspects of the spokesperson's communicative performance and to what extent the interventions denote preparation with media training strategies and techniques, with the purpose of obtaining the best results with risk and crisis communication. The study concluded that the voice as a government authority predominated in the interviews given to the media by the spokesperson for Civil Protection during the fires and floods (see Table 1) and that the verbal aspects of the preparation of her communication stood out compared to the nonverbal ones (see Table 2).

Keywords: verbal communication, nonverbal communication, framing, spokesperson, discourse analysis

1. Introduction

The effects of climate change can be felt across the Earth. Its consequences include intense droughts, water shortages, severe fires, rising sea levels, polar ice melting, catastrophic storms and reduced biodiversity. A report by the Intergovernmental Panel on Climate Change (Masson-Delmotte et al., 2021) emphasized that the Mediterranean region, in which Portugal is located, is especially vulnerable to extreme events resulting from climate change. In the country, these phenomena have taken place in urban areas, with intense and persistent precipitation, followed by floods, and, in rural areas, with large forest fires.

The fires of 2022 consumed 110 thousand hectares, the largest of which reached Serra da Estrela, with 28 thousand hectares burnt in eleven days (ICNF, 2022). Firefighting operations during the summer involved more than 12,000 operatives, 3,000 teams, 2,800 vehicles and 60 aerial firefighting aircrafts. Four people—two operatives and two elderly citizens—died as a result of the fires (SIC Notícias, 2022).

The rainfall in the Lisbon metropolitan region broke records in December 2022. Just between the 12th and 13th, rainfall reached 134.6 liters per square meter at the meteorological station of the Geophysical Institute in the Portuguese capital, the highest volume ever recorded at that station (Dias, 2022). The floods caused one fatality and affected millions of people. Insurance companies estimate that the economic losses exceed 18 million euros between insurances with houses, commercial establishments and vehicles (Afonso, 2022).

In charge of the operational response to natural disasters is the National Authority for Emergency and Civil Protection (ANEPC), a direct state administration body under the Ministry of Internal Administration. During the tragic rural fires of 2017, the then Second National Operational Commander of ANEPC and current Secretary of State for Civil Protection (SEPC), Patrícia Gaspar, became known as the spokesperson for the organization. Before taking on a political role in 2019, she accumulated over 20 years of experience in Civil Protection, which led her to aggregate two types of characteristics of spokespersons indicated in situations of risk and crisis: technical expertise and government authority. Patrícia Gaspar herself stated, when invited to join the Portuguese Government, her lack of political experience (Tavares-Teles, 2022). Therefore, we suppose the possible application of communicational strategies of media training that, throughout these three years as Secretary of State, contributed to developing her qualities as a spokesperson.

A study conducted by Gonçalves et al. (2021) revealed that Portuguese citizens believe technical expert spokespersons more than government authorities. Therefore, when it comes to contributing to risk perception and encouraging compliance with safety instructions, government communication should appeal to sources capable of promoting confidence concerning the capability of public organizations to respond to emergency situations. However, during a catastrophe, the dissemination of messages that aggregate technical and political information at the same time generates results not only in the population's behavior but also in organizational reputation (Olsson, 2014), which makes Patrícia Gaspar a potentially ideal spokesperson for our empirical study.

In this study, it is important to evaluate if during an emergency the Portuguese Civil Protection spokesperson addresses the population, through the media, as a technical expert or as a governmental authority. It is also of value to verify to what extent their interventions denote a preparation with media training strategies and techniques, with the purpose of creating more favorable conditions and making the best use of risk and crisis communication.

2. Literature review

2.1 Risk and crisis communication during natural disasters

Crisis and risk communication are specialized areas studied by public relations and strategic communication authors. Government public relations are a "weapon of power" (Cutlip, 1976, p. 5) defined as the "efforts to inform, interact with, influence, and protect multiple domestic and international publics in order to push forward democracy, serve public goods, defend human rights, and ethically gain public trust and support under normal and extreme circumstances" (Dong et al., 2023, p. 9). One of the research themes in government public relations is risk and crisis communication, which observes government communication and relationship management evolving risks, disasters and crisis responses, as well as political reputation repair. Once the public information model, characterized by one-way dissemination of information, is the model that predominates in government public relations activities (Grunig & Jaatinen, 1999; Valentini, 2013), the spokesperson performance is strictly relevant, especially in extreme situations.

Disaster communication represents an enormous challenge for public actors and organizations. Increasingly intense and frequent, the occurrence of disasters originating from climate change in various parts of the world reinforces the importance of a communication paradigm that contributes to ensuring the safety of the population ahead of protecting political reputation (Olsson, 2014). One of these paradigms is Crisis and Emergency Risk Communication (CERC). Developed by the Centers for Disease Control and Prevention (CDC), the agency responsible for health security in the United States, in 2002, as a result of the bioterrorist attacks after September 11. CERC was born as a manual and, over the years, has evolved into a model applied not only to public health issues but also to natural disasters and terrorism. Being prescriptive, its purpose is to facilitate communication planning and media relations during emergency situations in a large country with a federative organization, as is the case of the United States, which leads any risk and crisis management to involve a wide variety of agencies at national, state and municipal levels (Reynolds & Seeger, 2014; Sellnow & Seeger, 2013).

Within the scope of models specifically adjusted toward disaster communication, the IDEA Model (Sellnow et al., 2017) is focused on the design of effective instructional messages before and during high-risk events. At the message level, the purpose of IDEA is to assist recipients in internalizing the potential impact of the risk, offer a brief and intelligible explanation of the nature of the crisis and recommend a specific action. At the distribution level it is geared toward facilitating communication professionals to identify appropriate channels and strategies for message distribution. The tests conducted by the authors in the United States and Sweden found that the instructional message elaborated according to the criteria established in the IDEA model shows greater effectiveness in terms of self-protective behavioral intentions (Sellnow et al., 2019).

In relation to reputational aspects, according to the Situational Crisis Communication Theory (SCCT), forest fires and floods are a type of natural disaster that has public actors/organizations also as a victim of the crisis, implying weak attributions of responsibility and moderate reputational threat. Due to failures in prevention or insufficient means of combat, public actors and organizations can be blamed for the extent of damage from a natural disaster, which gives them strong attributions of responsibility and severe reputational threats (Coombs, 2019).

According to Yamori (2020), public organizations involved in natural disaster management are not able to establish a dialogue with citizens. They perform reactive communication for a passive population dependent on the information, often ambiguous, disseminated by government authorities. Part of this difficulty lies in the misunderstanding of the differences between the concepts of risk and crisis by communication professionals in the public context, which implies the need for different spokespersons and messages. Thus, the lack of preparation of spokespersons may compromise the effectiveness and, consequently, the quality of the communication disseminated. Occurring in a risk or crisis context, the consequences of unprepared communication can be aggravated for both the public and the reputation of those involved (De Waele et al., 2020).

2.2 Types of spokespersons in risk and crisis situations

A spokesperson is someone who publicly represents individuals or organizations. Their role is to convey information to the public or the media in order to ensure that the message is consistent and accurate. A spokesperson can also be someone whose messages are quoted in content produced by communication consultancies, or someone who lends their voice to endorse messages in journalistic content or advertising campaigns.

There are different types of spokesperson, depending on the type of organization, the type of crisis and the purpose of the communication. In any case, the ability to establish clear and effective communication is a crucial skill for a spokesperson. The technical specialist spokesperson is usually assigned because he or she has specific knowledge of a technical area and is thus able to provide accurate and reliable information on topics whose coverage is carried out by specialized journalists (Sánchez-Calero, 2006). The political authority type spokesperson is responsible for communicating the position of a political party, government or public organization to the media.

In communicating a natural disaster, technical experts voice messages about preparedness to address the upcoming risk and about relief and rescue operations. Political authorities, as far as they are concerned, are usually the most suitable spokespersons when the crisis has already been mitigated and the damage is being assessed (McLean & Ewart, 2015; Seeger et al., 2003; Sellnow & Seeger, 2013).

The spokespersons in natural disaster situations constitute a specific type. Their job is to ensure that accurate information about the event and safety measures are communicated clearly and in a timely manner to the public and the media. The spokespersons will relay critical information such as the extent of the disaster, the number of people affected and the organization's response. His/her role is to provide regular updates on the situation as well as safety instructions and recommendations to the public. Furthermore, he/she must also identify and correct false and inaccurate information that is circulating. A particularity of the spokesperson's role in disasters is the need to work closely with other organizations involved in the emergency response to ensure coordinated and consistent communication (Reynolds & Seeger, 2014).

The choice of who represents the ideas of an organization in the face of an audience during an emergency is a strategic decision that should consider the type of disaster in question, the message to be disseminated and the moment in the life cycle of the crisis. The designation of a single spokesperson can help the public assign a face to the event, contributing to the construction of the meaning of a crisis, but authors such as Littlefield and Cowden (2006) advocate the designation of multiple spokespersons to communicate with audiences from different cultural groups at times of crisis. In the mediatization process of natural disasters, the spokesperson of the public organizations involved take up a central role in the construction of the narrative about the event, reflecting the official positioning of the Executive Branch on the perception of risk, the framing of the crisis and the reality after the mitigation of the disaster (Lozano-Ascencio et al., 2017).

2.3 Media training and preparation of spokespersons

Media training aims to prepare spokespersons to interact with the media, to enable them to discuss with journalists in journalistic language (Mafei, 2008), but also to handle microphones and cameras, to understand what news is, to speak objectively and clearly, and to be direct in their communication. The objective of media training is to optimize the dissemination of information that, intermediated by the media, is directed to a lay or non-specialist audience (Assad & Passadori, 2009).

In the late 1980s, Fitzgerald and Wahl argued that, in order to mitigate misinterpretations or translations of medical jargon, health professionals should be trained in communication techniques (Araújo & Ruão, 2014). Also, authors dedicated to crisis communication recommend that spokespersons should turn to and adopt media training to engage with the media (Coombs, 2015), which many actually do. Two surveys conducted in U.S. organizations showed that almost 70 % of these provide preparation to their corporate spokespersons at least once a year (Lee, Woeste & Heath, 2007) and that this is the most common form of enablement in the context of crisis preparedness (Cloudman & Hallahan, 2006). Thus, media training should include strategies for interlocution in a crisis context to provide responses to tendentially negative and spectacularized media coverage (Lozano-Ascencio, Sánchez-Calero & Morales-Corral, 2017).

Despite the long temporal bridge that separates credibility, emotiveness and rationality of the discourse present in Aristotle's rhetoric (ca. 350 B.C./ 2018), this secular matrix remains for a successful verbal communication in contemporary times. Notably in crisis communication, this concept innovates with the inclusion of elements such as reputation, image repair, adequacy of the argument and persuasion to generate a discursive strategy that considers concerns, needs and motivations of the public (Benoit, 1995) for the self-defense of the organization in the face of a threat to its reputation (Gonçalves, 2011). In this logic and in the field of nonverbal communication, already in the middle of the last century the pioneer studies of the Palo Alto school identified seminal processes of personal interaction and established concepts such as the communicational paradox—as a contradiction between what is perceived by verbal and nonverbal communication—the universality of facial expressions of emotions (Ekman, 2003) or even the influence of the dimension of the space where the communication occurs, described in the theorization about proxemics (Hall & Schmid, 2007).

In the context of the communication of spokespersons with the media and the direct communication with the public, media training and communicative performance, especially in the dimensions of verbal speech and nonverbal communication, may be determinant in a more successful transfer of information. Moreover, different sources have different guidelines and focuses for this training. While research by Gorn et al. (2008) and Claeys and Cauberghe (2014) focused on content and some nonverbal aspects of communication, practical media training manuals devote more attention to verbal aspects of training (De Waele et al., 2020).

It also seems important to point out that research from disciplines outside communication sciences can add useful information. Experiments in Psychology show that when political speakers avoid critical questions during a debate—by answering a different yet similar question—the audience often misses the strategy and does not evaluate the speaker more negatively (Rogers & Norton, 2011), and these insights may offer an empirical basis for the use of interdisciplinary bridges.

3. Methodology

3.1 Research problem

This study aims to answer two research questions related to interviews granted by the Civil Protection spokesperson to the media during two specific risk and crisis situations that took place in the year 2022: the forest fires in Portugal and the floods in the Lisbon metropolitan region.

Research Question 1 (RQ1)—In the messages issued by the Civil Protection spokesperson, does the voice of the technical expert or that of the government authority predominate?

Research Question 2 (RQ2)—What media training strategies are identified—or absent—in the communication of the Civil Protection spokesperson with the media?

To answer these questions, we start with the following hypotheses:

Hypothesis 1 (H1)—The voice of government authority predominates in the interviews granted to the media by the Civil Protection spokesperson during fires and floods.

Hypothesis 2 (H2)—The verbal aspects of the communication of the Civil Protection spokesperson via the media stand out in relation to the nonverbal aspects.

3.2 Variables

This research is guided by the interpretative paradigm with the aim of identifying patterns in the Secretary of State's communications. To answer the research questions, we applied the qualitative method of discourse analysis (Daymon & Holloway, 2011), and examined four variables in the spokesperson's communications.

Variable 1 (V1)—Framing: An approach with a rhetorical perspective that involves the inclusion, exclusion and emphasis of certain information in a message (Hallahan, 1999). Thus, the choice of framing reflects the behavior the sender hopes to influence his audience with. This statement is in line with Hallahan's (1999) model of action framing, according to which the presentation of consequences in positive or negative terms influences an individual's behavior. Technical expert spokespersons tend to focus their messages on the harms (Seeger et al., 2003) that may arise from agreeing or refusing with guidance given by public actors and organizations, while political spokespersons more often address the positive consequences of the actions presented in their speeches.

Variable 2 (V2)—Audience: Technical experts tend to address their messages to a particular audience. In these cases, the target audience is addressed with verbs and pronouns in the second- and third-person singular (e.g., you, the citizen, each one). Messages issued by political spokespersons, on the other hand, are usually addressed to a universal audience, making use of second- and third-person plural (e.g., we, you, the population, everyone) (Seeger et al., 2003; Sellnow et al., 2009; Wang et al., 2022).

Variable 3 (V3)—Verbal communication: The use of soundbites—short sentences of immediate apprehension—is a communicative strategy developed in media training to increase the potential for retention of the message in the memory of the public from the diffusion of easily repeatable sequences. Also, the "translation" of expressions in language unintelligible to the general public, known as technical jargon, into colloquial language (Mateus, 2022) is one of the recommendations recommended in the preparation of spokespersons.

Variable 4 (V4)—Nonverbal communication: The media training manuals recommend that the spokesperson should always maintain firm and serene eye contact with his or her interlocutor to give him or her more credibility. Gaze aversion, therefore, consists in avoiding looking directly at the interviewer. Still in the nonverbal aspects of the training of spokespersons, the use of linguistic canes, with the use of phonetic elements without content, such as "ahhh" and "humm," is highlighted to be aware of this feature that can impair clarity (De Waele & Clays, 2017; Henningsen, 2005; Mateus, 2022).

3.3 Sample

The study sample is composed of eight videos (see Table 1) with interviews or statements of the Portuguese Civil Protection spokesperson, Patrícia Gaspar, published in the websites of the private Portuguese open television networks SIC Notícias and TVI. Regarding forest fires, we gathered five videos aired between

July 19 and August 19, 2022. Regarding floods, the three videos forming the sample cover the period between December 8 and 16, 2022.

Table 1. Samples's summary

Video	Date	Duration	Channel	Title	URL
A	19/07/2022	00:18:11	SIC Notícias	Interview with the Secretary of State for Civil Protection	https://bit.ly/3RNE4c6
B	30/07/2022	00:07:35	SIC Notícias	SIRESP failures: Secretary of State reinforces "operation and not network problems"	https://bit.ly/3VJxrst
C	30/07/2022	00:00:33	SIC Notícias	Secretary of State for Civil Protection reacts to SIRESP failures in Leiria fires	https://bit.ly/3L40Ybk
D	30/07/2022	00:01:28	SIC Notícias	Portugal will not return to alert status	https://bit.ly/3L739uY
E	19/08/2022	00:00:27	SIC Notícias	Country may be divided in the coming days between Alert and Contingency	https://bit.ly/3XNiN6a
F	08/12/2022	00:10:37	TVI	Bad weather: "We have no reason to talk about failures," says Secretary of State for Civil Protection	https://bit.ly/4cqH32I
G	14/12/2022	00:06:05	TVI	Bad weather in Lisbon: "Situation should worsen again tonight," but the scenario will not be so complicated	https://bit.ly/4eKKdzC
H	16/12/2022	00:01:00	SIC Notícias	Floods: Government explains why warning messages were not sent to the population	https://bit.ly/3VYItLM

Source: authors' own.

After sample collecting, the researchers carried out four rounds of video analysis, one round for each variable. The data and the researchers' impressions were recorded in a grid divided into four sections: video identification, discourse characteristics, media training aspects and researchers' notes.

4. Results

4.1 Framing

The analysis of the videos with the participation of the Civil Protection spokesperson, Patrícia Gaspar, shows, in relation to the framing variable, a more political than technical posture. In three of the eight videos, the message was focused exclusively on the positive consequences of the action referred to in the speech, for example, when the spokesperson announces that, since 2021, Civil Protection has invested in an increasingly preventive action: "The more we manage to join this dimension of self-protection with the work that is being done by the different institutions, the more resilience we will have and the more capacity we will have at the community level to react to these situations" (Video F). This framework can also be observed in Video C, in which the referred Secretary of State mentions that "the situation was promptly solved," when questioned by journalists about the defects in the Portuguese Integrated System of Emergency and Safety Networks (SIRESP) during the fires in Leiria; and in Video E, when she states that she has "a perfectly stabilised device that allows, and has allowed, to respond not only effectively, but also with great flexibility to the fires."

In one video only (Video A) we verified the existence of concomitant messages with positive and negative action framing. On the one hand, framed in the fact that the spokesperson stated that operations were running as planned with a satisfactory response from the emergency system, but that, even so, Civil Protection would reinforce the teams by hiring 500 more firefighters. On the other hand, focusing on the negative consequences of the action, the spokesperson appealed to the Portuguese not to stay in the forest areas and to avoid risky behavior under penalty of severe fires, as the climatic conditions made the fire spread very quickly.

The remaining four videos (Videos B, D, G and H) have no messages focusing on the consequences of action.

4.2 Audience

Regarding the audience variable, the analysis of the videos also reveals the predominance of the voice of the political authority over that of the technical expert, as in the eight videos in the sample, the spokesperson refers to a universal audience. The audiences mentioned by the spokesperson are, namely, "the Portuguese" (Videos A, F and G), "the communities" (Videos A and F), "the people" (Videos F and G), "the populations" (Videos F and G), "the immigrants" (Video B), "the tourists" (Video B), "the operatives" (Video B) and "the media" (Video G).

In six of the eight videos, Patrícia Gaspar uses the third-person plural (pronoun "we") to speak on behalf of the Portuguese Government (Videos, A, B, E, F, G and H). In three of the six videos, she uses verbal periphrases in the passive voice without explaining the agents of the action to answer the journalists' questions (Videos B, C and D), with expressions such as "it was clarified," "they were quickly resolved," "they should be implemented" and "the guidelines were given," these taken from Video C. In Videos F and G, the spokesperson also used the first person singular (pronoun "I"), which characterizes the emotive function of language, typical of political speeches.

In two videos, the Secretary of State takes advantage of her time with the media to call for safe behavior in emergency situations, but always addressing universal audiences, as when she asked "people to stay as much as possible at home, restricting movement in the street to what is absolutely necessary" in case of floods (Video G). Or when he addressed the Emigrante Chama campaign, reinforcing the alert and giving guidance on safe behavior in view of the high risk of fires (Video B).

4.3 Verbal communication

In three of the eight videos analyzed, the spokesperson uses soundbites such as "the challenge of a generation," "we have a real time bomb" or "Emigrante Chama,"[1] the title of the campaign aimed at Portuguese emigrants returning to their country of origin during the summer season.

Technical jargon was used in only two of the videos observed, with recourse to terms such as 'shadow zones,' a reference to territories where there were failures in operational communications and 'talk groups,' designations that refer to the technological structure of the communications network.

The main impressions we can draw from the spokesperson's verbal communication are the assumption, before the media, that technical explanations

1 'Chama' also translates to 'flame,' therefore with a dual meaning.

are not easy to provide and that "it is not possible to explain better" (Video B), with justification based on the very technical nature of the matter in question; and the use of negative adjectivation—such as, for example, "bad operation of telecommunications by the operatives" (Video B).

4.4 Nonverbal communication

In five of the eight videos, the spokesperson demonstrates gaze aversion (see Figure 1 and Figure 2), the most present attribute in her communicational performance and with a very significant expression: about 70 identified moments. Considering what was exposed in the literature review, this nonverbal aspect is usually associated with negative characteristics and/or behaviors of the spokespersons. The linguistic canes found, defined by De Waele and Clayes (2017) as a nonverbal vocal aspect of communication, are punctual and not very relevant, being present in only two of the eight analyzed videos and with low preponderance.

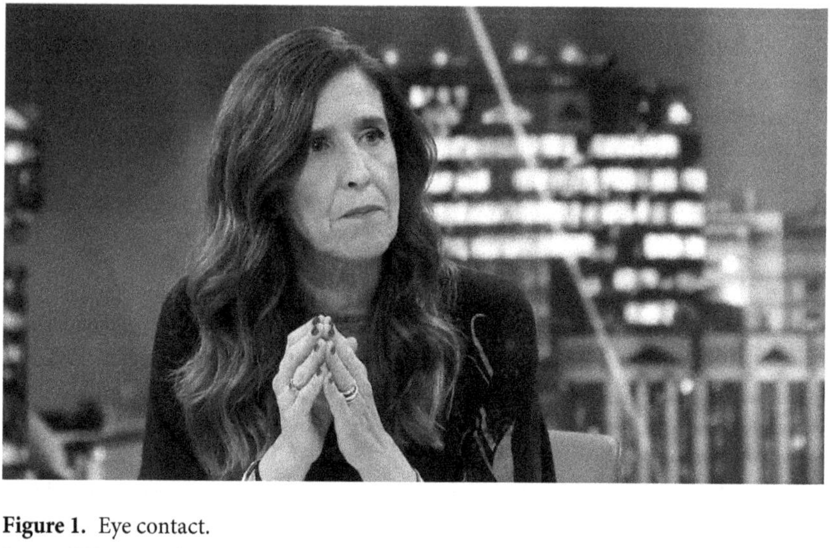

Figure 1. Eye contact.
Source: CNN Portugal.

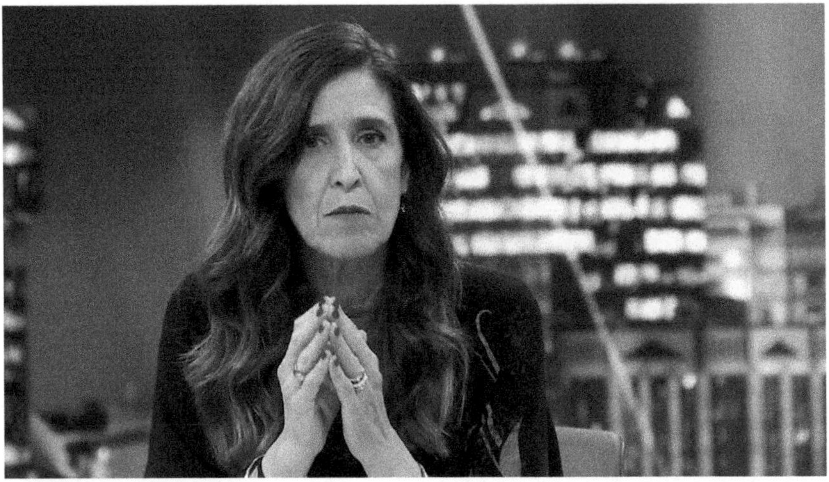

Figure 2. Gaze aversion.
Source: CNN Portugal.

As other relevant nonverbal communication aspects, we identified: occasional exaggerated gesticulation (see Figure 3); frequent sideways body movement, which may hinder the framing or be partially out of the plan; very present lateral head movements; body posture, when seated, tending to bend at the level of the shoulders; variable clothing, between casual and more formal and sober; interlacing of hands during questions from interviewers (denoting some uneasiness); interlacing of fingers during answers (a potentially distracting grimace); pointing at the subordinate in an apparent attempt to delegate the answers presented by the journalists; metallic sound resulting from the clash of rings when joining hands; on some occasions, the use of totally black clothing and hair tied up. One aspect that we considered particularly important was the facial expression, in the form of a very open and pronounced smile, when faced with questions raised by journalists in a tense interview context. This style was not constant, as there were communications in a more neutral tone and facial expression.

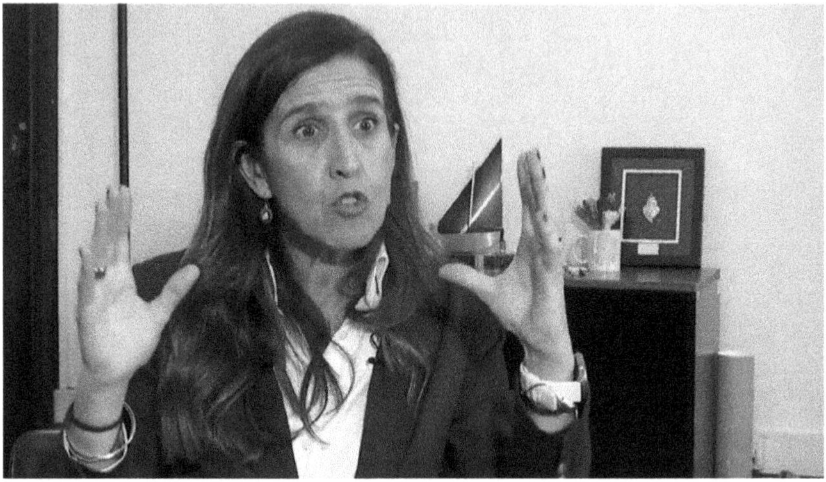

Figure 3. Vigorous gesticulation.
Source: SIC Notícias.

Table 2. Hypotheses and results

Hypothesis	Description	Result
H1	The voice of government authority predominates in the interviews granted to the media by the Civil Protection spokesperson during the fires and floods.	Confirmed
H2	The verbal aspects of the preparation of the communication of the Civil Protection spokesperson via the media stand out in relation to the nonverbal aspects.	Confirmed

Source: authors' own.

5. Discussion and conclusion

In this study, we assessed the speech of the Portuguese Civil Protection spokesperson, Patrícia Gaspar, during risk and crisis situations triggered by natural disasters of meteorological origin. Our objective was to verify which of the spokesperson profiles prevails in her communication given that she brings together two competences—technical and political—that are hardly found in members of the Portuguese Government (Silveira, 2022). We also discussed the Secretary of State's communicative performance and whether her interventions showed evidence of a preparation with media training strategies and techniques.

Regarding RQ1, the data led us to conclude that the voice of government authority predominated in the interviews given to the media by the Civil Protection spokesperson during the fires and floods, confirming H1. Thus, from the empirical study carried out, we believe that, in the face of situations of risk and crisis, in the communication, via the media, of a spokesperson who aggregates technical and political characteristics, the voice of the political authority will tend to prevail.

As we could observe in the videos that incorporate the sample, the Secretary of State speaks with property on technical issues concerning the operations, making permanent use of data, numbers and statistics. However, when questioned by a journalist (Video A) about the claimed success of a firefighting operation in Serra da Estrela, despite the catastrophic results of the rural fires in that region—30 % of the forest burnt down—the spokesperson was asked to respond as a technician, not a politician. The journalist asked her to explain in layman's terms how two such contradictory statements (success in the operation versus burning of huge forest area) could be considered positive in the Portuguese Government's assessment.

Corroborating our conclusion was the spokesperson's expedient to two reparative response strategies of the SCTT (Coombs, 2015). Oriented toward the negative effects on organizational reputation implied in crisis situations, the answers envisaged in SCTT are aligned with a political discourse, since the instructive and adjustment information, aimed at ensuring the physical and psychological safety of those involved, at the outset have already been given. Furthermore, we identified the following responses categorized by SCTT: reminds stakeholders that the organization is also a victim of the crisis and praises and/or thanks the work of other stakeholders involved.

In respect of RQ2, the data examined under the variables that reflect media training strategies point to an apparent limited preparation of the spokesperson, so it appears that the Secretary of State prepared herself for the interviews, hearings and statements under the focus of this study. The main gaps identified were the generalized absence of soundbites capable of synthesizing and optimizing the intelligibility of messages that were sometimes too technical and, almost always and given the context of a natural disaster; the inability to avoid excessive moments of gaze aversion when interacting with journalists, running the risk of a connotation with discomfort, distraction, deception or even lack of interest or involvement, shyness, anxiety. There are situations in which aversion to eye contact with the interlocutor is associated with disrespect, which is not at all evident in our observation. The use of technical jargon and linguistic canes is residual, which does not affect or condition the generality of the Civil Protection spokesperson's discursive performance.

Also, in the category of nonverbal communication, we observed a body posture that tends to be mobile, a factor that may denote some nervousness, but above all compromises the framing of the video, an aspect that, despite being technical, becomes unusual and distracting.

The nonverbal aspects of paralinguistics—such as timbre, tone of voice, volume, and rhythm—were not the object of this study, even though they may denote confidence, sarcasm, excitement, and hesitation, significantly affecting the perception and understanding of messages, besides conveying relevant contextual data, such as the emotional state of the spokesperson. However, given their relevance, we believe that they should be considered in future studies with a broader scope.

H2 is confirmed as from the perspective of the effectiveness and quality of communication of the Civil Protection spokesperson, the verbal attributes dominated over the nonverbal ones. The empirical study showed that the government spokespersons associated with media communication in risk and crisis scenarios are probably better prepared in terms of discursive strategies but demonstrate gaps in nonverbal preparation for the media clash and, ipso facto, lack capacity-building strategies, namely through media training.

In short, on the one hand, government communication professionals are faced with the challenge of making emergency communication more strategic, with planning based on important models (Coombs, 2019; Reynolds & Seeger, 2014; Sellnow & Seeger, 2013; Sellnow et al., 2017, 2019), to ensure a correct perception of risk and to guarantee the safety of the population. On the other hand, no less important is to promote trust in the authorities and the positive reputation of actors and organizations involved in managing the event, values that are fundamental to strengthen the adherence of the population to the instructions conveyed to them in situations of risk and crisis (Gonçalves et al., 2021). At this juncture, it is pertinent to channel government communication on disasters not only to the media but also directly to the population, through digital social networks, to establish a dialogue (Yamori, 2020), a closer communication that increases the degree of people's commitment to their safety in the event of disasters. At the message level, the appropriate use of the framings of action (positive or negative) according to the objectives, channels and audiences of the message are factors that contribute to the effectiveness of communication. At the audience level, different social groups are affected in different ways by disasters and, as we have seen in our study, spokespersons with political characteristics tend to direct their messages to homogeneous audiences, so an alternative is to designate spokespersons for varied communication objectives and audiences (Littlefield & Cowden, 2006). From the point of view of the preparation of spokespersons, the results led us to consider it important to clarify the panorama of media training practiced in Portugal and especially in the sphere of political and public communication. Training strategies remain a little explored, undervalued and possibly little discussed or mentioned topic in light of a certain social taboo.

The main limitations encountered in this study relate to the impossibility of comparing the performance of the Secretary of State in the interviews analyzed with others prior to the period of performance in office. This limited time window posed an additional difficulty: the size of the available sample (i.e., a number of videos that was less than desirable). Another limitation was the analysis restriction by the inexistence of other spokespersons conveying messages in the same context and with the same level of responsibility. Finally, we did not detect the presence of videos or even content from the spokesperson addressed directly to the population, through digital social networks and, therefore, without media intermediation.

References

Afonso, S. (2022, December 22). Seguradoras estimam pagar mais de 18,6 milhões pelas cheias em Lisboa. *Rádio Renascença*. https://bit.ly/3IBDwRm

Araújo, R., & Ruão, T. (2014). *A Comunicação estratégica na saúde: A relação de poder entre a assessoria de imprensa e o jornalismo*. In T. Ruão; R. Freias, P. Ribeiro, & P. Salgado (Eds.), *Comunicação organizacional e relações públicas: Horizontes e perspetivas. Relatório de um debate* (pp. 100–115). Centro de Estudos de Comunicação e Sociedade, University of Minho.

Aristotle. (2018). *Retórica*. Bertrand.

Assad, N. A., & Passadori, R. (2009). *Media training: Como construir uma comunicação eficaz com a imprensa e a sociedade*. Gente.

Benoit, W. L. (1995). *Accounts, excuses, apologies: A theory of image restoration strategies*. State University of New York Press.

Claeys, A. S., & Cauberghe, V. (2014). Keeping control: The importance of nonverbal expressions of power by organizational spokespersons in times of crisis. *The Journal of Communication*, *64*, 1160–1180. https://doi.org/10.1111/jcom.12122

Cloudman, R., & Hallahan, K. (2006). Crisis communications preparedness among US organizations: Activities and assessments by public relations practitioners. *Public Relations Review*, *32*(4), 367–376. https://doi.org/10.1016/j.pubrev.2006.09.005

Coombs, W. T. (2015). The value of communication during a crisis: Insights from strategic communication research. *Business Horizons*, *58*(2), 141–148. https://doi.org/10.1016/j.bushor.2014.10.003

Coombs, W. T. (2019). *Ongoing crisis communication: Planning, managing, and responding*. Sage Publications.

Cutlip, S. M. (1976). Public relations in the government. *Public Relations Review*, *2*(2), 5–28. https://doi.org/10.1016/S0363-8111(76)80001-X

Daymon, C., & Holloway, I. (2011). Discourse analysis and critical discourse analysis. In *Qualitative research methods in public relations and marketing communications* (pp. 178–192). Routledge.

De Waele, A., & Claeys, A. S. (2017). Nonverbal cues of deception in audiovisual crisis communication. *Public Relations Review*, *43*(4), 680–689. https://doi.org/10.1016/j.pubrev.2017.06.004

De Waele, A., Claeys, A. S., & Opgenhaffen, M. (2020). Preparing to face the media in times of crisis: Training spokespersons' verbal and nonverbal cues. *Public Relations Review*, Art. 101871. https://doi.org/10.1016/j.pubrev.2019.101871

Dias, D. (2022, December 13). Vivemos o dia de Dezembro em que mais choveu em Lisboa. *Público*. https://bit.ly/3Y49Kub

Dong, C., Zheng, Q., & Morehouse, J. (2023). What do we know about government public relations (GPR)? A systematic review of GPR in public relations literature. *Public Relations Review*, *49*(1), 1–13. https://doi.org/10.1016/j.pubrev.2022.102284

Ekman, P. (2003). *Emotions revealed: Recognizing faces and feelings to improve communication and emotional life*. Henry Holt and Co.

Gonçalves, G. (2011). *Narrativas de defesa e culpa nos discursos organizacionais*. In A. J. Palácios & J. Paulo Serra (Eds.), *Pragmática: Comunicação Publicitária e Marketing* (pp. 85–100). LabCom. https://bit.ly/3IVEg5a

Gonçalves, G., Piñeiro-Naval, V., & Persici Toniolo, B. (2021). Who do the Portuguese trust? Government communication management in the Covid-19 pandemic. *Comunicação e Sociedade*, *40*, 169–187. https://doi.org/10.17231/comsoc.40(2021).3251

Gorn, G. J., Jiang, Y., & Johar, G. V. (2008). Babyfaces, trait inferences, and company evaluations in a public relations crisis. *Journal of Consumer Research*, *35*(1), 36–49. https://doi.org/10.1086/529533

Grunig, J. E., & Jaatinen, M. (1999). Strategic, symmetrical public relations in government: From pluralism to societal corporatism. *Journal of Communication Management*, *3*(3), 218–234. https://doi.org/10.1108/eb026049

Hall, J. A., & Schmid, M. (2007). Sources of accuracy in the empathic accuracy paradigm. *Emotion*, *7*(2), 438–446.

Hallahan, K. (1999). Seven models of framing: Implications for public relations. *International Journal of Phytoremediation*, *21*(1), 205–242. https://doi.org/10.1207/s1532754xjprr1103_02

Henningsen, D. D., Valde, K. S., & Davies, E. (2005). Exploring the effect of verbal and nonverbal cues on perceptions of deception. *Communication Quarterly*, *53*(3), 359–375. https://doi.org/10.1080/01463370500101329

ICNF. (2022, October 17). *8.º Relatório Provisório de Incêndios Rurais*. Instituto de Conservação da Natureza e das Florestas. https://bit.ly/3KGEhel

Lee, J., Woeste, J., & Heath, R. (2007). Getting ready for crises: Strategic excellence. *Public Relations Review*, *33*(3), 334–336. http://doi.org/10.1016/j.pubrev.2007.05.014

Lozano-Ascencio, C., Sánchez-Calero, M. L., & Morales-Corral, E. (2017). *Periodismos de riesgo y catástrofes: En los telediarios de las principales cadenas de televisión en España* (182 pp). Fragua.

Littlefield, R. S., & Cowden, K. (2006, November 16). Rethinking the single spokesperson model of crisis communication: Recognizing the need to address multiple publics [Paper presentation]. *2006 National Communication Association Convention: Public Relations Division*, San Antonio, Texas, EUA. https://bit.ly/3kzRUS3

Mafei, M. (2008). *Assessoria de imprensa: como se relacionar com a mídia*. Contexto.

Masson-Delmotte, V., Zhai, P., Pirani, A., Connors, S. L., Péan, C., Berger, S., Caud, N., Chen, Y., Goldfarb, L., Gomis, M. I., Huang, M., Leitzell, K., Lonnoy, E., Matthews, J. B. R., Maycock, T. K., Waterfield, T., Yelekçi, O., Yu, R., & Zhou, B. (Eds.). (2021, in press). IPCC, 2021: Summary for policymakers. In *Climate Change 2021: The physical science basis*. Contribution of Working Group I to the Sixth Assessment Report of the Intergovernmental Panel on Climate Change. Cambridge University Press. https://bit.ly/3Z89QCu

Mateus, S. (2022). *Manual prático de assessoria de imprensa*. LabCom. https://bit.ly/3IWyRuF

McLean, H., & Ewart, J. (2015). Hindrance or help? A model for the involvement of politicians in communicating with publics during disasters. *International Journal of Mass Emergencies and Disasters*, *33*(2), 228–252. https://doi.org/10.1177/028072701503300205

Olsson, E. K. (2014). Crisis communication in public organisations: Dimensions of crisis communication revisited. *Journal of Contingencies and Crisis Management*, *22*(2), 113–125. https://doi.org/10.1111/1468-5973.12047

Reynolds, B., & Seeger, M. (2014). *Crisis and emergency risk communication*. U.S. Department of Health and Human Service, Centers for Disease Control and Prevention. https://bit.ly/3m80fwH

Rogers, T., & Norton, M. I. (2011). The artful dodger: Answering the wrong question the right way. *Journal of Experimental Psychology: Applied, 17*(2), 139. https://doi.org/10.1037/a0023439

Sánchez-Calero, M. L. (2006). *La información especializada en la gestión de crisis*. Fragua.

Seeger, M. W., Sellnow, T. L., & Ulmer, R. R. (2003). *Communication and organizational crisis*. Praeger.

Sellnow, D. D., Lane, D. R., Sellnow, T. L., & Littlefield, R. S. (2017). The IDEA Model as a best practice for effective instructional risk and crisis communication. *Communication Studies, 68*(5), 552–567. https://doi.org/10.1080/10510974.2017.1375535

Sellnow, D. D., Johansson, B., Sellnow, T. L., & Lane, D. R. (2019). Toward a global understanding of the effects of the IDEA Model for designing instructional risk and crisis messages: A food contamination experiment in Sweden. *Journal of Contingencies and Crisis Management, 27*(2), 102–115. https://doi.org/10.1111/1468-5973.12234

Sellnow, T. L., & Seeger, M. W. (2013). *Theorizing crisis communication*. Wiley.

Sellnow, T. L., Ulmer , R. R., Seeger, M. W., & Littlefield, R. S. (Eds.). (2009). *Effective risk communication: A message-centered approach*. Food Microbiology and Food Safety Series. Springer.

SIC Notícias. (2022, September 30). *O balanço da época mais crítica de incendios em Portugal este ano*. https://bit.ly/41wweqs

Silveira, P. (2022). *O Governo de Portugal. Ensaios da Fundação*. Fundação Francisco Manuel dos Santos.

Tavares-Teles, A. (2022, July 26). Patrícia Gaspar: na linha de fogo. *Notícias Magazine*. https://bit.ly/3Z6oPws

Valentini, C. (2013). Public relations in the public sector: The role of strategic communication in the Italian public administration. *Sinergi Rivista di Studi e Richerche, 92*, 93–113. http://doi.org/10.7433/s92.2013.06

Wang, Y., Kim, J., Chatham, A., & Ma, L. (2022). "I lose" "I gain" vs. "They lose" "They gain": The influence of message framing on donation intentions in disaster fundraising. *Journal of International Crisis and Risk Communication Research, 5*(1), 29–56. https://jicrcr.com/index.php/jicrcr/article/view/62

Yamori, K. (2020). *Disaster risk communication: A challenge from a social psychological perspective*. Springer.

Alejandro Álvarez-Nobell, Gabriel Sadi, and María Belén Barroso

Effective leadership in public relations in Latin America: The role of empathy for employee engagement

Abstract: During COVID-19 and in response to the demands of younger generations, many leaders in organizations could have changed their communication style and humanized the way they interact. This paper aims to understand the role of empathy in communication leadership and its effect in the work environment for Latin American PR practitioners. This study relies on several theories that suggest that the ability to have and show empathy is an important part of effective and servant leadership (Spears, 2002). Empathy enables leaders to show individualized levels of consideration to followers (e.g., Avolio & Bass, 1995), recognize the emotions of others (Rubin et al., 2005) and be aware of both self and context (Walumbwa et al., 2008). In addition, empathic communication allows leaders to connect with and respond to different stakeholders (Dolamore, 2019). Measures of empathy are adapted from the Emotional Competence Inventory (Boyatzis et al., 2000). A survey dataset has been collected from practitioners in 20 Latin American countries (N = 1,345), using SPSS for data analysis. The results show an increasing projection of empathy levels, and a correlation between the application of empathy in communication leadership and employee engagement.

Keywords: internal communication, employee engagement, emphatic leadership, Latin America

1. Introduction

During COVID-19 and also in response to the demands of younger generations, many leaders in organizations have changed their communication styles and humanized the way they interact. They show empathy when connecting with their teams, trying to understand their feelings and emotions, putting themselves in the other's shoes and taking an active interest in their concerns. The increase in empathy in communication could affect the work environment of communication professionals. Additionally, many organizations now encourage flexible, remote, and collaborative working in real time for interaction.

In Europe, recent studies (Zerfass et al., 2022) show that a large majority of professionals have experienced a strong increase during the pandemic in empathetic attitudes by their communication leaders. Specifically, those leaders have been (1) concerned about the personal well-being of others and have shown sensitivity and understanding, (2) have identified team members' strengths and limitations, and (3) have been paying attention to their team members with good listening skills. Based on these results, the study in Europe correlates with a greater commitment of employees to their organizations and their work. Indeed, professionals who work with an empathic leader are significantly more engaged and committed, especially in a communication department or agency.

This chapter aims to analyze and understand the role of empathy in communication leadership and its effect on the work environment of Latin American public relations professionals. In doing so, it also aims to confirm the trend already demonstrated in Europe and thus be able to foster the development of these leadership skills and team culture in the Latin American region.

2. Theoretical framework

Changes in personal relationships inside and outside organizations have been strongly affected by the current crisis. Uncertainty, pressures and strong emotions seem to be key dimensions in any organization. From the field of public relations and internal communication, contributions have been made that can help minimize this uncertainty (Li et al., 2021) and positively affect the well-being of employees (Sinčić et al., 2020). Similar efforts have been also made regarding the need for organizations and their leaders to focus their attention on internal communications, improving the support they receive and having employees identify more strongly with their organizations (Wills-Espinosa et al., 2017).

A determining factor for leadership in communication is to generate a climate of trust (Pološki et al., 2020) and commitment, and allow employees to reach the private sphere, for example, in health matters (Lee & Li, 2020). At the level of positive communication, it has already been shown (Álvarez-Nobell et al., 2012; Muñiz-Velázquez & Pulido, 2019) that cultural development in organizations is strongly linked to leadership, especially in relation to the internal management of informal and intra-organizational communications in coordination with formal communication (Aced-Toledano et at., 2022; Cuenca & Verazzi, 2020; Cuenca-Fontbona et al., 2022; Tkalac et al., 2012) In turn, the ethical dimension in internal communication is also a transcendental factor (Mubarok & Darmawan, 2019).

Leadership in the realm of communication can be linked to empathy (Cropanzano et al., 2017; Jian, 2022; Kellett et al., 2006; Sadri et al., 2011; Watkins et al., 2019), defined as the act of "putting oneself in someone else's shoes" to understand their perspective. Empathetic leaders demonstrate a genuine understanding of their followers' thoughts and feelings, with empathy being an essential component of effective leadership and service (Figueras, 2021; Moya, 2016; Spears, 2002). This ability enables them to display a personalized level of consideration for their followers, as noted by Avolio and Bass (1995), in addition to recognizing others' emotions (Rubin et al., 2005) and maintaining self-awareness and awareness of the context in which they operate (Walumbwa et al., 2008). Certainly, it is important to understand that these elements vary depending on the culture and, therefore, are interpretable in different ways according to each individual's culture. That is why cultural intelligence is crucial for the observer to recognize the signals from the observed person. In this way, the observer can convey empathy to the observed person correctly (Hall, 2023).

Empathic communication allows leaders to connect and respond to diverse stakeholders (Dolamore, 2019), also aiding them in strengthening their commitment to their teams and organizations (Tao et al., 2022). It is worth noting that there are tools for measuring empathy, such as scales based on the Emotional Competence Inventory developed by Boyatzis et al. (2000). The result could be a more symmetrical internal communication scenario that positively predisposes to change by enhancing the cognitive and affective skills of employees (Sun et al., 2021), allowing the organizational commitment of their team to be strengthened by leaders (Meyer & Allen, 1997).

The research questions of this study are as follows:

RQ1: How does the level of perceived empathy vary between leaders?

RQ2: Is there a correlation between the application of empathy in communication and employee engagement?

3. Methodology

An online questionnaire in Spanish and Portuguese was used, which corresponds to the 2022/2023 edition of the Latin American Communication Monitor (LCM). The LCM is a biennial longitudinal survey created by a research partnership of 34 universities in the Americas and Europe, organized by the European Public Relations Education and Research Association (EUPRERA) and the Global Communication Monitor series. The questionnaire is based on research problems and hypotheses derived from 15 years of experience and previous studies, with 21 questions that were grouped into the section dedicated to the topic of empathy and leadership and demographic ones as well. The instruments used in the answers are dichotomous, nominal and ordinal scales.

After the adjustments indicated in a pre-test (which was carried out with 86 representative persons on a professional, age and geographical scale), invitations to participate in the study were sent to 37,220 practitioners. The questionnaire was started to be filled in by 2,740 professionals from 20 Latin American and Caribbean countries, and was completed by 1,134, which constitutes the sample with representative profiles at the demographic level and in the type of organizations in which they work. Demographic data reveal the high quality of the sample, which was dominated by senior professionals with a strong qualification base and long tenure in the field. The mean age was 41.5 years.

Regarding the sample construction, in order to be representative and comparable across different countries, it follows the international standards established globally and discussed in contributions such as those by Moreno and Humanes (2009). In this regard, we work with a sample dimension that is directly related to the sampling error and, therefore, to the confidence intervals of the study. Concerning the sampling type, while the ideal approach is to conduct a fully probabilistic sample (simple random sample), it is common to use stratified or clustered samples. Another factor to consider is the non-response rate, for which a minimum acceptance of 70 % is attempted. These sample design patterns are consistent in both the overall study and the sub-samples from each country (Athaydes et al., 2022).

The Latin Communication Monitor (LCM) is considered representative in its country-specific samples for several reasons. Firstly, the number of "representative" responses for each country in Latin America has been calculated using various sources, such as the size of Social Sciences graduates in Latin America according to UNESCO, the total responses per country from the last LCM 2020 survey, and the total users who visited the website within a specific period. Additionally, a confidence level of 90 % and a sampling error of 10 % have been established. The results indicate that a representative sample of respondents should be close to 40 individuals based on both the mean and median values. Therefore, it can be stated that the LCM has a sample that approaches the standards of statistical representativeness in the region.

The online data collection instrument was active for 12 weeks between August and October 2022 in a dedicated website, which allowed participants to access other research-related data and previous reports. The answers corresponded to the perception and assessment that the respondents had on the selected topic based on their knowledge or theoretical and empirical approaches.

The responses of the participants who did not fit the profile required in the research were excluded from the database. 13 Latin American and Caribbean countries have achieved statistically representative data for nominal comparative purposes (Colombia, Argentina, Bolivia, Uruguay, Costa Rica, Chile, Mexico, Venezuela, Ecuador, Brazil, Peru, Puerto Rico and the Dominican Republic) (see Table 1). Finally, the analysis was based on 95 % valid responses from communication professionals currently active in the region.

Table 1. Response rate of major markets (countries included in the comparison)

Country	Region	Respondents	Percent
Brazil	South America	149	13.1
Colombia	South America	141	12.4
Argentina	South America	125	11.0
Uruguay	South America	94	8.3
Bolivia	South America	91	8.0
Chile	South America	87	7.7
Costa Rica	Central America	87	7.7
Mexico	North America	64	5.6
Venezuela	South America	55	4.9
Ecuador	South America	51	4.5
Peru	South America	47	4.1
Puerto Rico	The Caribbean	41	3.6
Dominican Republic	The Caribbean	40	3.5

Source: LCM 2022/2023.

The statistical analysis of the data was done in November and December 2022 with SPSS, software recognized for the precision of its calculations and its versatility to visualize the results.

In addition, cluster analysis will be carried out to classify and correlate variables, and universally accepted coefficients will be used: Chi^2, ANOVA / Scheffé Post-hoc-Test, independent samples *t*-test, Pearson correlation or Kendall rank correlation (Significant results are marked with *($p \leq 0.05$, significant) or ** ($p \leq 0.01$, highly significant) in the graphics or tables).

4. Results and discussion

The profile of strategic communication and public relations professionals in Latin America shows that 35.4 % of the respondents are unit leaders or managers of a single discipline in a communication department; 62.5 % of them have more than ten years of experience in communication management; 63 % of all respondents are women; and the vast majority (92.7 %) of the sample has an academic degree.

Half of the respondents work in communication departments of organizations (5 % public limited companies; 18 % private companies; 15 % state entities, public sector, political organizations; 9 % non-profit organizations), while 52 % work for a consulting firm or are freelancers.

Regarding the research questions, when inquiring about the empathy levels of leaders or supervisors, the results of the study indicate high level and increasing projection in leader empathic communication: 81.3 % strongly agree that their leader is empathetic toward their team, and 77.1 % say that this situation has increased in the last year (see Figure 1).

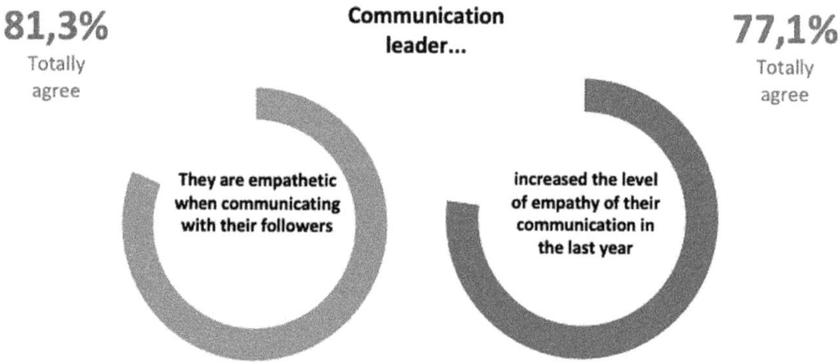

Figure 1. Empathy levels of communication leaders
Source: LCM 2022/2023.

When we delve deeper into the analysis of the situations that determine this increase in empathy on the part of communication leaders, the results of the study highlight, in order of importance: (1) Pays attention and listens well (79.8 % agree or strongly agree); (2) Cares about the personal well-being of others and shows sensitivity and understanding (79 %); and (3) Identifies other team members' strengths and limitations (78.7 %).

The least valued factor is that the leader "accurately assesses the underlying causes of a person's problems" (67.4 %). Consequently, it is possible to find high to moderate attention levels regarding the problems of my team (see Figure 2).

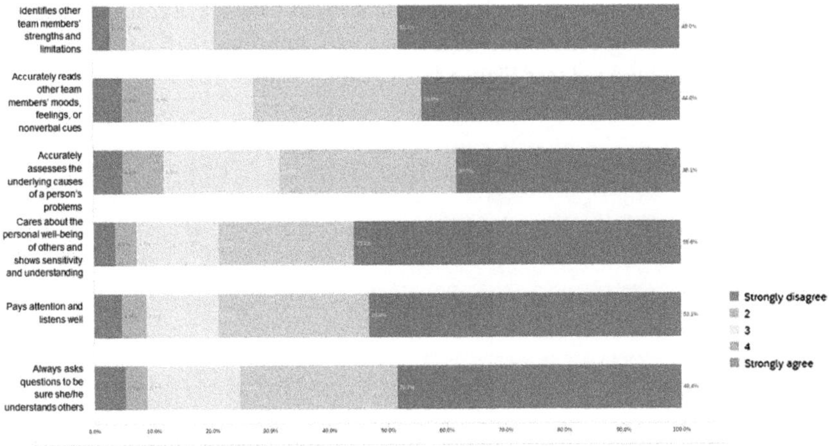

Figure 2. Characteristics of empathetic leadership in communication.
Source: LCM 2022/2023.

It is also worth noting that there is a significant difference across organizations, with agencies/consulting firms having more empathetic leaders than the other ones (see Figure 3).

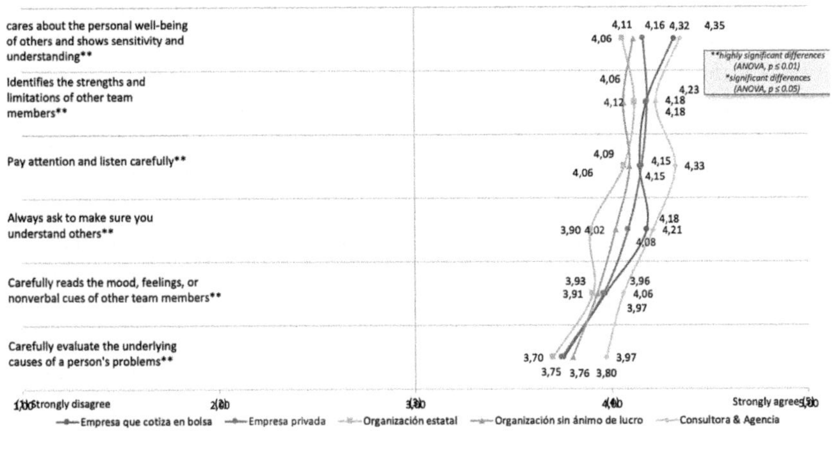

Figure 3. Empathic leadership across organizations.
Source: LCM 2022/2023.

Finally, when analyzing the self-assessment of daily work as a communication practitioner, a strong commitment (low burnout, importance of work, no need to change) is highlighted (see Figure 4).

Figure 4. Perceptions of daily work from communication practitioners
Source: LCM 2022/2023.

Four related dimensions are analyzed to enable a comparison between empathic and non-empathic leaders in the communication profession in Latin America and thus shed light on the second research question. Organizational commitment being the first one, measured with three items: "working at my organisation has a great deal of personal meaning to me" (72.8 % agree or strongly agree), "I have a strong sense of belonging to my organisation" (69.1 %) and "I feel personally attached to my organisation" (65.6 %).

The second dimension is work engagement, measured with three items as well: "I am enthusiastic about my job" (84.2 % agree or strongly agree), "I am immersed in my work" (81.2 %) and "At my work, I feel bursting with energy" (74 %).

The third element is mental health, and its three items for measurement purposes are as follows: "I can effectively solve the problems that arise in my work" (86 % agree or strongly agree), "I do not doubt the significance of my work" (71.7 %) and "I do not feel used up at the end of a workday" (56 %).

Finally, as for the fourth dimension, it is related to turnover intention, and 30.2 % of the respondents agree with the statement regarding their intentions to change jobs during the next year. Figure 5 illustrates the four dimensions and evidence that the type of organization plays an important role: consultancy and agency staff report higher engagement, better mental health and lower turnover than those working in internal departments in organizations.

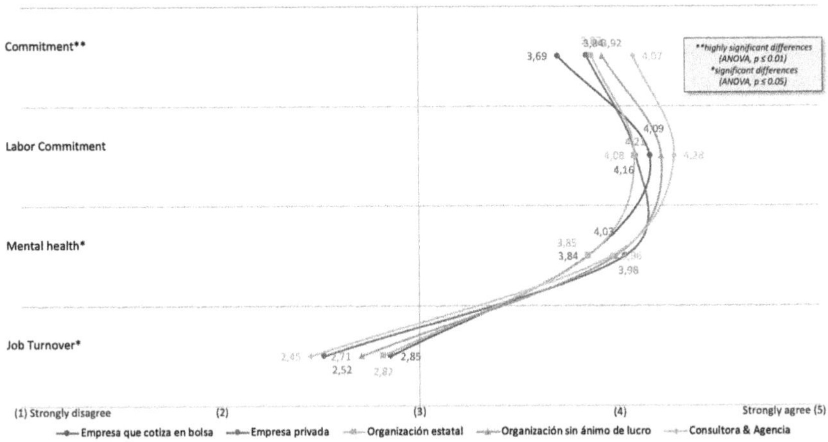

Figure 5. The four dimensions in professionals working in different organizational types.
Source: LCM 2022/2023.

So, summarizing, the findings show that Latin American communication practitioners overall are committed to their organizations and generally highly engaged by their work. Regarding mental health, considering the impact that the COVID-19 pandemic has left in the matter, there is evidence relating to the fact that many communicators feel tired from their work, but the vast majority feel able to handle their jobs despite the weight of these demands.

In relation to differences by gender, women appear more likely to indicate less engagement to their work (4.30 against 4.15 from their male counterparts, considering mean values of indices), with no statistically significant differences regarding organizational commitment, mental health and turnover intentions.

In the final version of the paper, a detailed analysis of these results will be carried out, detailing aspects related to the type of organization, the functions of the professionals, their gender and their alignment with the standards of excellence of the communication departments.

As for the second research question, a correlation between the variables associated to the application of empathy in communication and employee commitment has been found, which establishes a basis for further discussion about its implications. Either way, as it can be seen in Figure 6, the most relevant differences in favor of empathic leadership can be observed in three dimensions, organizational commitment, work engagement and turnover intentions, while in the mental health dimension the differences between having an empathic leader and not seem less significant.

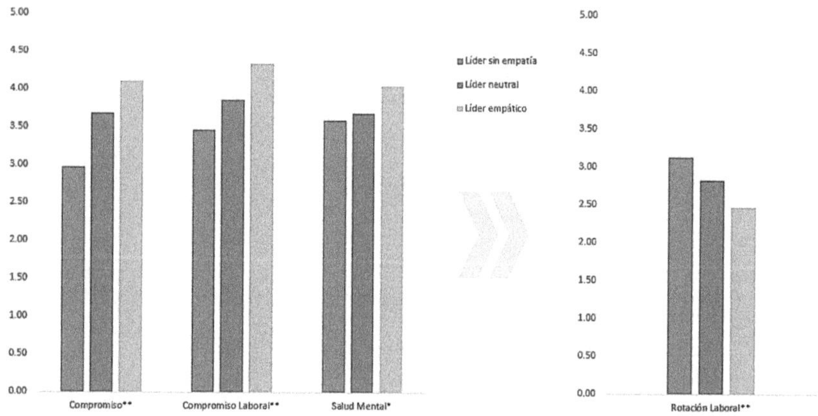

Figure 6. The four dimensions in relation to empathic and unempathic leaders.
Source: LCM 2022/2023.

In any case, these results from Latin America show a somewhat important difference with its European counterpart (Zerfass et al., 2022). Indeed, in Europe, the differences between working for an empathic leader or not in a communication department or agency are significantly higher, particularly in relation to turnover intentions.

5. Conclusion

What happens with public relations in a society marked by risk, uncertainty, insecurity and economic, social and environmental crisis? Although internal communication is a dimension that is increasingly shared with areas of "people management," the contributions from the perspectives of well-being and purpose are increasingly important for our disciplinary field.

As already pointed out, the changes that we are experiencing in how organizations face the situation and the way of relating between the various internal publics is changing. In other words, the role of internal communication in organizations seems to have been highlighted during the pandemic.

A repeated factor is the need to strengthen empathy, close and emotional communication and the role of leaders. All this is making it possible to reduce uncertainty and increase employee commitment.

The results of the study provide valuable insights into the two research questions at hand. Firstly, regarding RQ1, the findings demonstrate that the level of perceived empathy varies between leaders in the communication profession in Latin America. A significant majority of respondents strongly agree that their leaders are empathetic toward their teams, indicating a high level of perceived empathy among leaders. This suggests that there is a positive perception of empathetic leadership within the profession, highlighting the importance of empathy as a leadership trait.

Secondly, addressing RQ2, the study establishes a correlation between the application of empathy in communication and employee engagement. The findings reveal that leaders who demonstrate empathetic communication practices are associated with higher levels of organizational commitment, work engagement, and reduced turnover intentions among employees. This correlation underscores the significance of empathy in driving employee engagement and fostering a positive work environment. It implies that empathetic leaders who actively listen, show concern for personal well-being, and recognize individual strengths and limitations create an atmosphere that enhances employee engagement and commitment.

Overall, these findings emphasize the varying levels of perceived empathy among leaders and highlight the positive correlation between empathy in communication and employee engagement. They underscore the importance of fostering empathy as a leadership attribute and its potential impact on employee outcomes, ultimately contributing to the overall success and well-being of organizations in the Latin American context.

This study, and similar European studies already mentioned, begin to provide evidence toward the importance of empathy in communication leadership and could promote communication and public relations departments to make decisions in this regard. Indeed, an empathic leader in communication teams relates to better organizational and work commitment and better mental health levels, so that could be a strong argument for developing empathic leadership competencies and team culture all over Latin America.

5.1 Limitations and future directions

The focus of this study and its analysis only corresponds to one of the five sections of the LCM, so participant fatigue may have negatively affected data quality. A large sample of professionals was approached, but a relatively small number initiated and completed the online questionnaire, which led to the underrepresentation of some countries in the region in the comparative analysis. In the future, a greater participation would be desirable to allow a more complete comparative analysis, that is, integrating more countries.

Regarding future research opportunities, comparative studies between Latin American countries or with other Global Communication Monitor studies (from Europe, Asia-Pacific, or North America) that have analyzed the topics could be interesting to investigate similarities and differences between the regions, and thus contribute to deepening the understanding of the relationship between empathy and communication leadership on a global scale.

References

Aced Toledano, C. A., Segarra, S. M., & López-de-Ayala, M. C. (2022). The impact of the Covid-19 pandemic. The perception of communications executives in companies: The role and challenges of internal communication. *Anàlisi, 67*, 27–43. https://doi.org/10.5565/rev/analisi.3559

Álvarez-Nobell, A., Romero-Calmache, M., Sánchez-Sanvicente, M., & Aragües-Dufol, P. (2012). Organizational culture development. A study model based on the grounded theory method. *Revista Mediterránea de Comunicación, 3*(2), 111–127.

Athaydes, A., Álvarez-Nobell, A., & Molleda, J. (2022). Latin American Communication Monitor: estrategia metodológica para un macroestudio de alto impacto académico y profesional en el continente. In L. Marroquín (Ed.), *Comunicación en Contextos Socioorganizativos, Aportes Teórico—Metodológicos* (pp. 161–174). CICOM. https://cicom.ucr.ac.cr/wp-content/uploads/2022/11/Comunicacion-En-Contextos-Sociorganizativos-Aportes-Teorico-Metodologicos.pdf?fbclid=IwAR2uz9pTS6prfM9vTuP7FmaHjrAZxta6V4wilZjuNOp3txAxkzWthMwksnU

Avolio, B. J., & Bass, B. M. (1995). Individual consideration viewed at multiple levels of analysis: A multi-level framework for examining the diffusion of transformational leadership. *The Leadership Quarterly*, 6, 199–218. https://doi.org/10.1016/1048-9843(95)90035-7

Boyatzis, R. E., Goleman, D., & Rhee, K. (2000). Clustering competence in emotional intelligence: Insights from the Emotional Competence Inventory

(ECI)s. In R. Bar-On & J. D. A. Parker (Eds.), *Handbook of emotional intelligence* (pp. 343–362). Jossey-Bass.

Cropanzano, R., Dasborough, M. T., & Weiss, H. (2017). Affective events and the development of leaders-member exchange. *Academy of Management Review, 42*(2), 233–258.

Cuenca, J., & Verazzi, L. (2020). *Comunicación interna total: estrategia, prácticas y casos.* Editorial UOC.

Cuenca-Fontbona, J., Compte-Pujol, M., & Sueldo, M. (2022). The function of internal communication during the COVID-19 health crisis: Transformation or transubstantiation? *Anàlisi, 67*, 7–26. https://doi.org/10.5565/rev/analisi.3553

Dolamore, S. (2019). Detecting empathy in public organizations: Creating a more relational public administration. *Administrative Theory & Praxis, 43*(1), 58–81. https://doi.org/10.1080/10841806.2019.1700458

Figueras, C. (2021). La mitigación en los discursos de salud mental. In S. Ridao & Y. González (Eds.), *Estudios filológicos y lingüísticos. Homenaje el Profesor Manuel Peñalver.* Comares.

Hall, A. C. (2023). Comunicación intercultural y sensibilidad empática en el liderazgo empresarial. *Círculo de lingüística aplicada a la comunicación, 93*, 165–178.

Jian, G. (2022). From empathic leader to empathic leadership practice: An extension to relational leadership theory. *Human Relations, 75*(5), 931–955.

Kellett, J. B., Humphrey, R. H., & Sleeth, R. G. (2006). Empathy and the emergence of task and relations leaders. *The Leadership Quarterly, 17*(2), 146–162.

Lee, Y., & J. Y. Q. Li. (2020). The value of internal communication in enhancing employees' health information disclosure intentions in the workplace. *Public Relations Review, 46*(1), Art. 101872. https://doi.org/10.1016/j.pubrev.2019.101872

Li, J. Y., Sun, R., Tao, W., & Lee, Y. (2021). Employee coping with organizational change in the face of a pandemic: The role of transparent internal communication. *Public Relations Review, 47*(1), Art. 101984. https://doi.org/10.1016/j.pubrev.2020.101984

Meyer, J. P., & Allen, N. J. (1997). *Commitment in the workplace: Theory, research and application.* Sage.

Moreno, Á., & Humanes, M. L. (2009). Limitaciones y riesgos de la investigación transcultural en Relaciones Públicas y Comunicación estratégica. El auge de las macroencuestas. *Revista Latina de comunicación social, 64*, 52.

Moya-Albiol, L. (2016). *La empatía en la empresa.* Plataforma Editorial.

Mubarok, E. S., & Darmawan, J. (2019). The influence of training, motivation, and work ethics on the internal communication and their impact on the employee performance. *European Journal of Business and Management, 11*(24), 86–93. https://doi.org/10.7176/EJBM/11-24-10

Muñiz-Velázquez, J. A., & Pulido, C. M. (2019). *The Routledge handbook of positive communication: Contributions of an emerging community of research on communication for happiness and social change*. Taylor and Francis.

Poloski, N., Rimac, M., & Naijar, D. (2020). Building organizational trust through internal communication. *Corporate Communications: An International Journal, 26*(1), 70–83. https://doi.org/10.1108/CCIJ-01-2020-0023

Rubin, R. S., Munz, D. C., & Bommer, W. H. (2005). Leading from within: The effects of emotion recognition and personality on transformational leadership behavior. *Academy of Management Journal, 48*, 845–858. https://doi.org/10.5465/amj.2005.18803926

Sadri, G., Weber, T. J., & Gentry, W. A. (2011). Empathic emotion and leadership performance: An empirical analysis across 38 countries. *The Leadership Quarterly, 22*(5), 818–830.

Sincic, D., Poloski, N., & Tkalac, A. (2020). Does good internal communication enhance life satisfaction? *Journal of Communication Management, 24*(4), 363–376. https://doi.org/10.1108/JCOM-11-2019-0146

Spears, L. (2002). Tracing the past, present, and future of servant-leadership. In L. Spear & M. Lawrence (Eds.), *Focus on leadership: Developments in theory and research* (pp. 1–16). Palgrave Macmillan.

Sun, R., Li, J. Y. Q., Lee, Y., & Tao, W. (2021). The role of symmetrical internal communication in improving employee experiences and organizational identification during Covid-19 pandemic-induced organizational change. *International Journal of Business Communication, 60*(4), 1398-1426. https://doi.org/10.1177/23294884211050628

Tao, W., Lee, Y., Sun, R., Li, J. Y., & He, M. (2022). Enhancing employee engagement via leaders' motivational language in times of crisis: Perspectives from the Covid-19 outbreak. *Public Relations Review, 48*(1), 102133.

Tkalac, A., Vercic, D., & Sriramesh, K. (2012). Internal communication: Definition, parameters, and the future. *Public Relations Review, 38*(2), 223–230. https://doi.org/10.1016/j.pubrev.2011.12.019

Walumbwa, F. O., Avolio, B. J., Gardner, W. L., Wernsing, T. S., & Peterson, S. J. (2008). Authentic leadership: Development and validation of a theory-based measure. *Journal of Management, 34*, 89–126. https://doi.org/10.1177/0149206307308913

Watkins T., Fehr, R., & He, W. (2019) Whatever it takes: Leaders' perceptions of abusive supervision instrumentality. *The Leadership Quarterly*, *30*(2), 260–272.

Wills-Espinosa, N., Cevallos, M. I., Sadi, G., & Ancin, I. (2017). La relación entre la satisfacción con la comunicación interna y el compromiso organizacional. El caso de una universidad ecuatoriana. *Austral Comunicación*, *6*(1), 133–160. https://doi.org/10.26422/aucom.2017.0601.wil

Zerfass, A., Moreno, A., Tench, R., Vercic, D., & Buhmann, A. (2022). *European Communication Monitor 2022. Exploring diversity and empathic leadership, CommTech and consulting in communications. Results of a survey in 43 countries*. EUPRERA/EACD.

Part Two Institutional Communication and Institutional Relations

Joan Cuenca-Fontbona, Marc Compte-Pujol, Mariana Sueldo, and Ramon Martin-Guart

A public relations perspective on communication challenges in public institutions

Abstract: Public institutions face challenges that require increasingly professional communication approaches. In addition to daily service and local agendas, they must address supra-local issues such as globalization, economic recovery, ecological awareness, and technological development. Tensions between short, medium, and long-term considerations, aligned with the relational and reputational paradigm, result in certain professional gaps. Drawing from literature focused on institutional communication within the realm of public relations and conducting interviews with communication managers in local public administrations with populations ranging from 10,000 to 20,000 inhabitants in the province of Barcelona, this chapter aims to analyze the praxis of communication service in municipalities. These services aim to enhance transparency, good governance, and public access to information while outlining their communicative function within their organizational structures. Findings from this approach reveal that communicative functions within the local public sphere are multidisciplinary and lack research-driven decision-making. The approach tends to be tactical and primarily anchored in informative functions, management of owned organic channels, and media relations techniques or publicity. Consequently, there is a lack of orientation in communication departments of these institutions toward a strategic direction specialized in public relations.

Keywords: public administration, Barcelona, corporate communication, Dircom (Director of Communication), strategy, public relations

1. Introduction

Since the early twentieth century, public relations have played an increasingly significant role in the public sector, encompassing a wide array of institutions and organizations funded by public taxes, existing to serve a public purpose. Beyond central, regional, and local governments, the public sector also includes publicly funded healthcare and education, the military, the police, firefighters, ambulance services, and often a complex web of partnerships designed to coordinate the work of different public sector entities (Kinnear, 2022). Public administrations, by their very nature, are committed to communication and must consider communication as a strategic tool integrated into all institutional decisions (Canel, 2018; Moreno-Sardà et al., 2017).

In Spain, the obligation to inform and communicate is outlined in Article 69.1 of Law 7/1985, of April 2, regulating the bases of the Local Regime of 1993 (García-Gordillo & Pérez-Curiel, 2021, p. 35). Additionally, it stems from the approval of the Transparency, Access to Public Information, and Good Governance Law (Law 19/2013 of the Government of Spain and Law 19/2014 of the Autonomous Community of Catalonia).

In this legal context, such organizations are required to be accountable to society. Society must know how public funds are used, what they produce, and how they benefit the public. Public administrations are expected to provide information that prioritizes rigor, precision, and transparency over any other interests (Bertot et al., 2010; Molina-Rodríguez-Navas et al., 2021; Rodríguez-Navarro et al., 2017; Zerfass et al., 2019). To achieve this, information must be complete and understandable to ensure democratic participation in public affairs by all citizens (Moreno Sardà et al., 2013, p. 524).

Due to their public service orientation, public administration must strive to build trust with the citizenry (Kim & Lee, 2012; Schmidthuber et al., 2020; Tolbert & Mossberger, 2006). Hence, the practice of public relations, capable of contributing to the generation of intangible values such as trust and engagement, is fundamental and indispensable in the communication practice of these institutions (Canel & Luoma-aho, 2017, p. 45; Castillo-Esparcia et al., 2020; Cuenca-Fontbona & Puentes-Rivera, 2019: 7). In fact, as L'Etang (cf. Kinnear, 2022) explains, the origins of the public relations profession can be traced, in part, to government press agencies. Furthermore, communication with all internal and external strategic stakeholders is the primary duty of any public administration. This communication also serves to reinforce brand identity, the strategic and differential value of intangible assets, and consequently, the image and reputation of the institution (García-Gordillo et al., 2021, p. 32; Kinnear, 2022, p. 433; Rodrich Portugal, 2012).

In the context of local public institutions, public relations represent a significant tool that allows government teams to explain, justify, and legitimize their political decisions, demonstrating their commitment to transparency and enhancing the institution's credibility in the collective imagination (Paricio-Esteban et al., 2019). In the words of Haywood (1991, cf. Kinnear, 2022, p. 430): "The reality is that the more transparent the government, the better the service it provides, and the more responsive the authority… the more important the quality of public relations support becomes."

For this research, we aim to examine whether the communication function of a representative sample of local public administration in the province of Barcelona, Spain, aligns with the strategic planning process and the ideals of communication bidirectionality as conceived within the academic discipline of public relations.

2. Theoretical framework

In Spain, numerous studies have emerged concerning the management of communication and public relations in municipal communication departments or offices across autonomous communities such as Andalusia, Aragon, the Canary Islands, Catalonia, the Community of Madrid, the Valencian Community, Galicia, and Navarre. The majority of these works tend to focus on the analysis of the more traditional function of institutional communication: the informative aspect (Gértrudix et al., 2016; Manfredi-Sánchez et al., 2017; Moreno Sardà et al., 2013, 2017; Paricio-Esteban & Bruno-Carlos, 2018; Rodríguez-Breijo et al., 2021, among others). Conversely, there are limited works that shed light on other functions of municipal communication, such as its role in facilitating citizen participation (Paricio-Esteban et al., 2019; Simelio & Molina-Rodríguez-Navas, 2014).

In this study, we conceptualize municipal public administration management from the managerial perspective of public relations (Compte-Pujol, 2016; Cutlip et al., 2012; Grunig, 1992). We consider two of its key theoretical contributions: Grunig and Hunt's relational models (1984) and Marston's strategic planning process in public relations (1963, cf. Matilla, 2018).

2.1 Systemic theory and models in public relations

During the 1980s and 1990s, James Grunig and his colleagues conducted extensive quantitative surveys in America, Asia, and Europe as part of what became known as the Excellence Project (Dozier et al., 1995; Grunig & Hunt, 1984). Rooted in systemic theory, this research aimed to create balance and harmony between organizations and their publics through public relations. It resulted in the synthesis of four relational models initially, later expanded to five (see Table 1). These models have been considered paradigmatic within the field of public relations studies and strategic communication in general, albeit not without theoretical controversy (Falkheimer & Hiede, 2018, p. 39).

Table 1. Five models for public relations

	Publicity model	**Information model**	**Asymmetric two-way model**	**Symmetric two-way model**	**Game model—mixed motive**
Aim	Propaganda	Dissemination of information	Scientific persuasion	Mutual understanding	Negotiation win-win
Process	One-way truth not essential	One-way truth important	Two-way truth important	Two-way truth important	Two-way perspective
Model	Sender-receiver	Sender-receiver	Feedback system	Group-to-group network	Sender-sender
Effect	Exposure	Distribution	Range attitudes	Qualitative understanding	Diplomatic agreement

Source: Falkheimer and Heide (2018), adapted from Grunig and Hunt (1984) and Dozier et al. (1995).

Models have emerged at different times in history, with the publicity model being the oldest and the game model the last to appear, and all of them can coexist today in the professional practice of public relations management, depending on the purpose of the organization and the context in which it finds itself (Grunig, 1992). For example, the publicity model, which represents the first period of the profession's practice in the United States, is still used in certain contexts, especially in the entertainment industry or in certain political situations.

The first two models (publicity and public information) are often used by organizations that have a dominant view of their environment and do not see communication as relational, but merely as the transmission of predetermined rules and messages. Two-way models allow audiences in the organizational environment to exert some influence, but within the terms of the organization.

In the context of public administrations, beyond " information" campaigns, which involve one-way communications (sender-receiver) that would fit mainly in the public information model, " communication" campaigns, which involve two-way communications (sender-receiver-sender), should also be addressed, especially when it comes to persuading citizens to change their behavior or opinions, for example in relation to maintaining a healthier lifestyle (Kinnear, 2022: 423). Such campaigns, whose core is science-based persuasion (with prior research to determine the best way to persuade), have the characteristics of the two-way asymmetric model.

As suggested by authors such as Kinnear (2022), the increasing responsibility of the public sector to engage with stakeholders through transparency and consultation should facilitate the rise of two-way asymmetric communication or even two-way symmetric communications. Citizens no longer see themselves as mere recipients of information, but as co-creators of the services they receive, and they want to be treated as such by their institutions (Canel & Luoma-aho, 2018).

In this sense, Fedorico et al. (1991, cf. Kinnear, 2022, p. 430) stress that in a local government environment it is especially important that communication is not merely a one-way propaganda, but a two-way flow of communication between "…those you want to talk to and those you want to listen to."

2.2 Strategic planning in public relations

The first author to establish the strategic decision-making process adapted to the discipline of public relations was John Marston in his book *The Nature of Public Relations* (1963), and he structured it in four stages which he called RACE (Research, Action, Communication and Evaluation), also known as the spiral method. He was inspired by the classic management process of management by objectives and his proposal is still today one of the most widely used models in the professional development of the communication function in organizations (Matilla, 2018, p. 40).

Practically all the authors of manuals on the discipline of public relations use the strategic planning process for public relations as a basis (Wilcox et al., 2015), although they may differ in the name and even the number of phases, but the result is always the same: a public relations project begins by investigating the situation, continues with the development of a diagnosis on which to establish goals and objectives based on a strategic approach, continues with the planning and implementation of actions that respond to the objectives, and concludes by evaluating whether these objectives have been met, if they have not been evaluated throughout the process (Xifra, 2014, p. 123).

There is unanimity in the fact that in order to carry out a correct communication with current and potential audiences, the organization must first research them exhaustively in the first phase of the strategic planning process (Cuenca, 2018; García-Gordillo & Pérez-Curiel, 2021; Oliveira, 2018). Only in this way will the institution be able to generate "calm, thoughtful and contemporary responses" to its needs (Rodrich Portugal, 2012).

Among the many communication tools and channels available to the communication management of local councils, Web 2.0 resources stand out above all others, as they offer public administrations the possibility of disseminating information about their management and encouraging citizen participation in projects, initiatives and services offered in the municipal agenda (Álvarez-Nobell et al., 2017; Bonsón et al., 2012, 2015; Campillo-Alhama & Martínez-Sala, 2017; Criado & Villodre, 2020; Graham & Avery, 2013; Guillamón et al., 2016; Lev-On & Steinfeld, 2015; Marcos García et al., 2021; Moon, 2002; Ohme, 2018; Reddick et al., 2017; Solito & Materassi, 2020). The multiplicity of social media accounts makes it possible to establish a dialogue with each target audience in particular and with society in general. Institutions can speak in the first person and address the outside world without external mediators, a function developed to date by traditional media (García-Gordillo et al., 2021; Thorson et al., 2020).

Each social network has its own narrative, its own specificities and, as a consequence, its audiences. Gaining notoriety, maintaining the appreciation and loyalty of audiences and conveying the value of the image that one wants to consolidate in a context totally dominated by social media requires the development of social media strategies.

Finally, it should be noted that the effectiveness of the application of the RACE method (or similar subsequent methods) in professional practice will depend on whether the values of two-way communication are clearly integrated into the public relations policy of the organization in question (Matilla, 2018, p. 41). Likewise, its implementation will also be strongly conditioned by the valuation that top management gives to the public relations function within the organization or, in other words, whether it categorizes it as a philosophy (strategic orientation) or as a function (exclusively tactical orientation) (Matilla, 2018). This conception can be easily detected from the structure and performance of the communication and public relations department in each organization.

2.3 The structure of the municipal communication department and the profile of the person in charge of it

At the structural level, the communication departments of public administrations are currently usually directly dependent on the highest institutional position—at the municipal level, we would speak of the mayor's office—and occupy the same level as the rest of the members of the government team (García-Gordillo & Pérez-Curiel, 2021). These directorates are considered as integrated parts of the organization's top management scheme and are committed to and involved in strategic decision-making processes.

The main function of the communication management of a local administration is to design and implement a global communication strategy that represents the public institution (Campillo-Alhama & Martínez-Sala, 2017; García-Gordillo & Pérez-Curiel, 2021). Their function goes beyond the role of mediator before the media and goes beyond the traditional duties that defined the heads of press offices that do not respond to strategic objectives, planned in order to achieve and evaluate results (Almansa, 2011; Espino González, 2022). It must turn its communication department into a cohesive entity of the municipality, offering truthful, plural and transparent service information, being an informative reference for citizens, fostering public debate for participation, and promoting civil society and associations (Bel-Mallén, 2004, cf. Paricio-Esteban et al., 2019).

3. Objectives

The main objective of this research has been to check whether the communication function of the sample of local public administrations explored is aligned with strategic and two-way communication applied to public relations.

This study was based on three research questions (RQs):

RQ1. How are the communication departments of these municipalities structured and to whom do they report?

RQ2. Are the municipalities' communication plans designed following the four-stage strategic public relations planning process (research, planning, implementation and evaluation)?

RQ3. What are the communication actions and the media ecosystem of local councils to communicate with their strategic audiences?

Finally, a project hypothesis has been determined:

H1. The communication departments of local councils contemplate in their praxis the strategic approaches of public relations.

4. Methodology

Firstly, the literature specializing in public relations and corporate communication was reviewed, specifically that which deals with communication in public administration, in order to ascertain the state of the art of this function in these institutions. Then, a semi-structured interview (Corbetta, 2003; Gillham, 2005) was designed, tested and proposed to a sample of experts with an eminently professional profile, since they are people who manage and/or carry out tasks directly related to the model object of the research, that is, they have the power to strategically design communication actions and plans and, therefore, can contribute their experience and reflective capacity on the profession.

4.1 Sample

The interview was conducted by videoconference, within the framework of distance research methods (Lichtman, 2006), between the months of May and December 2022, using a sampling approach of n=18 functional heads of communication from a universe of N=30 that make up 60 % of all the town councils of towns with between 10,000 and 20,000 inhabitants in the Spanish province of Barcelona, which, due to their high level of representativeness, constitute a quality sample.

The sample of this research focused only on the areas of communication. At this point, it should be clarified that, although the functional area capable of dealing with communication is referred to as the communication department, there is a complete lack of homogenization in the name of the department.

4.2 Questionnaire and qualitative analysis

For the elaboration of the interview, a Mini-Delphi (Landeta, 2006) was designed and carried out with the participation of five experts, including professionals and academics in this area of knowledge. The profile was determined according to three criteria: (a) they had more than five years of experience; (b) they were reputed experts in the public sector (heads of communication departments in public entities, company directors or members of national and international research teams in academic institutions), and (c) they had a broad knowledge of the discipline and the realities of the public sector.

The interview was derived from the objectives and the research questions and followed the phases of interview development: the interview script was prepared, the questionnaire was pilot-tested with three people, refined, and then the 18 interviews were conducted for 1 hour each, followed by transcription. Finally, the information was analyzed and a preliminary report was written.

The questionnaire included 32 questions organized into three blocks linked to the research questions and hypotheses, which allowed for ordering and subsequent comparison in order to extract the results. The first section asked for information on the structure and performance of the communication department. The second section called for reflection on strategic aspects of communication. The last module focused specifically on the media ecosystem and communication actions (Table 2).

Table 2. Public service communication in local authorities

Research questions	Questions in the questionnaire	Type of question
RQ1. How are the communication departments of these municipalities structured?	What is the name of the communication area?	General answer option
	What is the name of the position of the person responsible for communication?	General answer option
	What is the educational background of the person responsible for communication?	Fixed response alternatives
	How many people work in the communication area?	
	What is the position of communication in the council organigram?	
	Does the communication area work with the support of an external agency/consultant?	
	What is the usual role and responsibilities of the communication area?	
	How is the communication department organized?	General answer option
	What is the public's impression of the council's communication management?	Fixed response alternatives
	What is the budget of the communication department?	Fixed response alternatives
RQ2. Are the municipalities' communication plans designed following the four-stage strategic public relations planning process (research, planning, implementation and evaluation)?	What is the element of the communication process that is most taken into account when designing a communication action?	General answer option
	Of all the functions of the communication service, to which is most time devoted?	General answer option
	Is the municipal communication plan coherent with the Municipal Action Plan, PAM, or Municipal Investment Plan, PIM?	Fixed response alternatives
	Is there a municipal communication plan?	Fixed response alternatives
	Is there a municipal internal communication plan?	Fixed response alternatives
	Is there a municipal vulnerability, risk and crisis communication plan?	Fixed response alternatives
	Is preliminary research undertaken to be able to design the municipal communication plan (actions)?	Fixed response alternatives

(*continued*)

Table 2. Continued

Research questions	Questions in the questionnaire	Type of question
	What environmental opportunities are being taken advantage of in terms of communication?	General answer option
	What environmental threats are being taken into account by communication?	General answer option
	What unique features of the municipality are reported?	Fixed response alternatives
	What are believed to be the main concerns/ interests of the population?	Fixed response alternatives
	What kind of communication actions or plans are designed?	Fixed response alternatives
	What is the intentionality of the municipal communication plan being designed?	Fixed response alternatives
	What is the style of the contents of the municipal communication plan that are disseminated?	Fixed response alternatives
	What is the predominant format of the content published in the municipal communication plan?	Fixed response alternatives
	What are the audiences of the municipal communication plan?	Fixed response alternatives
	What kind of segmentation of strategic audiences is done?	Fixed response alternatives
	Are the main processes of the communication department automated?	Fixed response alternatives
	By which indicators is the municipal communication plan evaluated?	Fixed response alternatives
RQ3. What are the communication actions and the media ecosystem of local councils to communicate with their strategic audiences?	What internal channels and actions are used and what is the frequency of content updates and usage?	Fixed response alternatives
	Which external channels and actions are used and how often is the content updated and used?	Fixed response alternatives
	In general, what is the reach, impact, level of saturation, level of personalization, visibility, usage and cost (correlation between the communication effort and the reception sought) of the communication channels?	Fixed response alternatives

Source: authors' own.

The three stages of quantitative and qualitative content analysis were then deployed: pre-analysis, exploitation of the material using Atlas.ti, and processing the results to make them meaningful and allow interpretations to be formulated (Shaw, 2003; Silverman, 2006). This analysis was carried out by two researchers in collaboration, to ensure stability and inter-observer reliability (Krippendorf, 1990; López-Aranguren, 1989).

5. Presentation of results and discussion

5.1 The communication department of local public administration

First of all, if we look at the name of the communication departments, we can see in Table 3 that, of the 18 institutions interviewed, the divergence in the name allows us to question their responsibilities and whether these departments are a functional or strategic area in the institution's organizational chart.

Table 3. Names* of communication departments

Communication section	1
Communication	2
Communication, institutional relations and external projection	1
Communication and information management	1
Communication and protocol	1
Communication and ICT	1
Information and communication department	1
Communication Department	3
Press Department	1
Communication office	2
Image and communication	2
Press and communication service	1
Communication service	1

Source: authors' own.

*Terms to refer to the department in charge of the communication function

Similarly, the names of the positions that head these departments are not homogeneous, with the most common name in a public call for proposals being that of Communication Technician. The others, as can be seen in Table 4, have different names, depending on whether they have been assigned other competences unrelated to communication, such as management of the transparency portal, the electronic headquarters, support for citizen participation activities, or some administrative functions or those of another department.

Table 4. Job title of the person responsible for communication

Communication and ICT Coordinator	1
Head of Mayor's Office and communication	1
Head of communication and protocol	1
Head of the Mayor's Office and communication	1
Head of press and communication	1
Head of communication	1
Head of communication, new technologies and transparency	1
Communication assistant technician	1
Communication technician	5
Communication and institutional relations technician	1
Communication and information management technician	1
Education, youth and communication technician	1
Communication and citizen participation technician	1
Communication, transparency and participation technician	1

Source: authors' own.

The professional profile of the people responsible for this functional area is directly conditioned by the qualifications required by the public calls for applications for this type of department, which are usually degrees in journalism, advertising and public relations or audiovisual communication (García-Gordillo & Pérez-Curiel, 2021). The higher academic education and previous professional experience of the reference person may also be determining factors. This research shows that 15 of the communication managers in the Barcelona city councils studied have a university degree in journalism (83 %) and the remaining 3 have a degree in advertising and public relations (17 %). It is worth noting that none of these people have postgraduate studies specializing in communication or, specifically, public relations. In three cases, they have postgraduate studies related to public administration management.

In general, the communication departments of these types of entities are small, with 1 person (48 %), 2 people (23 %), 3 members (10 %) or more than 3 (19 %). When the communication department is larger, it is because it is also responsible for municipal radio or local television.

In terms of their position and hierarchical dependence in the organization chart of the City Council, 13 of the communication departments interviewed are attached to the Mayor's Office (72.2 %), 4 report to both the Mayor's Office and a councilor's office which, among other responsibilities, also has responsibility for communication (22.2 %), and 1 is attached to what is called the City Council's Autonomous Media Organisation (OAMC),[1] which is the public body in charge of municipal communication (5.6 %).

There are also 13 local councils that have an external agency or freelance staff (72.2 %) who, on a one-off basis, provide support, above all in creativity and design, in the production of graphic materials, and in the management and optimization of the digital ecosystem of organic media.

The list of functions and responsibilities of the department includes citizen service communication, digital communication (web, App, newsletters, municipal magazines and social networks), supervision of content design and creativity, design and production of institutional advertising (offline), communication of municipal reputation and prestige, institutional merchandising, planning of advertising media, production of materials (print, audiovisual, offline, etc.) and relations with the media (Table 5).

All the municipal communication departments coincide in offering a transversal service of assistance to the different areas of the council according to their needs. The organization and structure of the communication service is conceived from the contents that are created and the communication channels that are managed. The communication referents are responsible for the website and the municipal social networks, mainly Twitter, Instagram and Facebook and, if the council has one, also for the municipal App. They are in charge of news and the public agenda, with varying frequency depending on the council, the municipal newsletter or magazine which, in addition to being offered in digital format, usually has paper print runs ranging from 1,800 to 3,500 copies, depending on the municipality, distributed in citizens' mailboxes and also in municipal facilities, through the postal service or by hiring freelance staff. They also produce and distribute, according to the municipality, other communication elements such as yearbooks or calendars, etc. In addition, more than half (55.5 %)

1 An Autonomous Media Organisation (OAMC) is a municipal institution supervised by a City Council and constituted in the exercise of the powers of self-organization by the same City Council, in a decentralized regime and in the form of a local autonomous organization of an administrative nature in accordance with the Law Regulating the Bases of Local Regime.

of the communication departments reinforce, on many occasions, the citizen attention office, the OAC, and the actions and festivities that require specific communication campaigns. The interviewed referents also offer support to events and their protocol, which are usually promoted, according to them, by councils such as Economic Promotion, Culture, Education and Youth or Tourism.

The heads of the institutional communications departments are satisfied with their work and think that the population gives a rating close to a "B" (6.92) to the municipal communications service they receive.

Table 5. Roles and responsibilities of the communication department

Communicating with the public	**Fa**	**Fr (%)**
Social Responsibility policy communication	12	66.6
Vulnerability and risk communication and crisis communication	1	5.5
Digital communication	18	100
Internal communication	18	100
Marketing plan design	6	33.3
Design and creativity	1	5.5
Design and production of materials and institutional advertising (offline/ online)	18	100
Spokesperson training	7	38.9
Identity, image, reputation, prestige, legitimacy and	4	22.2
municipal positioning (city brand)	18	100
Institutional merchandising	9	50
Organization of events and protocol	11	61.1
Organization of or participation in trade fairs and congresses	2	11.1
Advertising media planning	18	100
Media relations	18	100
Institutional relations	10	55.5

Source: authors' own.

n = 18 professionals respond (multiple response) about roles and responsibilities.

The budgets available to the communication departments amount to between 5,000 and 60,000 euros per year. The main expenses are the publication and printing of the municipal bulletin or magazine, diaries, yearbooks or calendars. Other notorious costs are external collaborators and the production of graphic and audiovisual materials, etc. The municipalities with higher communication budgets respond to items that are allocated to the maintenance of the local radio or television stations they are in charge of.

5.2 The strategic plan (actions) of municipal communication

The consulted referents understand that they should, and do not, pay attention to what the bibliography on strategic communication sets out: preliminary research, strategic planning, operational mechanics and, in particular, final evaluation indicators. All agree that the elements of the communication process that are most taken into account are those that require the function to be rigorous, in line with the classic literature on communication: clarity, conciseness and style of content and the most appropriate formats and channels. In fact, the entire sample details that all of their time is concentrated on writing content and managing channels such as the website, social networks, municipal magazines and newsletters or the App.

A prior question, a prelude to any strategic approach, and on which there is no unanimity among the heads of the sample analyzed, is that not all the institutional communication plans or actions that are drawn up are consistent with the municipal action and investment plans, the PAM and the PIM[2] (66.6 %). Some of the referents express that only some of the actions are related (28.6 %), and only one of them indicates that the communication task is not coherent with the municipal action plan (4.8 %).

61 % of the institutional communication departments in the sample do not work on the basis of any communication plan, but rather on the basis of a series of communication actions that provide coverage for the different municipal communication needs. The remaining 39 % say that they do have a communication plan, which at the time was designed with the support of Barcelona Provincial Council, but confess that they have either never applied it or have done so only partially. They also state that these communication plans are obsolete and should be updated. No communication department has an internal communication plan, nor does it have a vulnerability, risk or crisis communication plan.

The data show that the majority of professionals claim that they do not outline communication actions based on any kind of preliminary research (77.7 %). Few use some kind of quantitative analysis of communication actions or an opinion poll, taking advantage of spaces for citizen participation (22.3 %), to make decisions. Likewise, and in order to understand the factors on the basis of which they carry out their function, they were asked about the opportunities and threats in the environment that influence them. And, on the one hand, the results

2 The PAM is the acronym for the municipal action plan and the PIM is the acronym for the municipal investment plan.

reveal important similarities in the opinions expressed by the professionals in the communication departments with regard to taking advantage of the opportunities offered by the macro-environment. Next generation aid, feminism, equality and diversity, protection of the biosphere and the environment, communication of the Sustainable Development Goals, the Sustainable Development Goals-SDGs, and sustainability in general, working and collaborating in the community and proximity model, and movements related to the city brand, are the topics that are being incorporated into the agendas of council government teams and, likewise, in the dissemination tasks of these institutional communication departments. On the other hand, the communication departments are concerned about disinformation and fake news, low trust in public administration and politics in general on the part of citizens, and issues on the supra-municipal public agenda such as cultural diversity, safety, cleanliness and hygiene, harassment, vulnerability or social exclusion.

The issues of this municipal environment that are communicated are recurrently related to trade and economic development, cultural heritage and popular festivals, education, geography and history of the municipality, sports, facilities and technological development, the image and reputation of the municipality and tourism. In addition to all issues related to local government action plans such as road works and maintenance, employability, land management, social services and housing and public aid.

They were then asked about the concerns and interests of citizens in order to be able to correlate them with the issues disseminated by the council. In all the cases studied, there was agreement on the importance given by the population to housing and public spaces, facilities and basic services (61.9 %), education, urban improvement and public safety (52.4 %), health and social welfare, and culture and sports (47.6 %), street cleaning and infrastructure (38.1 %), environment and economic development (28.6 %), employability (23.8 %), equality, inclusion, social cohesion and participation (19 %), migratory movements and the rural environment (14.3 %) and, to a lesser extent, technological development (4.8 %).

Institutional communication actions are mainly designed to raise awareness and educate (100 %), while protecting the image and reputation of the institution (83.0 %) and the municipal environment (57.1 %), to report on municipal news and social services (42.9 %), to support the marketing function in offering municipal services (38.1 %), in the field of institutional relations (33.3 %), and to support social actions (19 %). And, although it has already been mentioned that no council has an internal communication plan, 28.6 % of the respondents insist that they systematically inform public employees via email, at the same time as external communication is deployed.

With regard to the communicative intentionality of municipal communication actions, a certain divergence can be observed in the opinions of the professionals surveyed. For all of them, any action is designed to inform (100 %), for others the aim is to build loyalty (47.6 %), educate and/or dialogue (38.1 %), or engage (33.3 %) strategic audiences. Recognizing (28.6 %), influencing (19 %), persuading strategic audiences (14.3 %), or entertaining (9.5 %) would be other basic functions.

The journalistic style (100 %) is the one that dominates in all the contents of the communication actions that are carried out, followed by advertising (19 %) and public relations (9.5 %). In addition to current affairs (100 %), the most frequently used genres are those specific to the journalistic profession: agendas (95 %), chronicles (81 %), interviews (76.2 %), reports (66.7 %) and opinion articles and content curated (38.1 %). It is explained that the use of photography and images, graphics and infographics is used whenever necessary (95 %).

Worth mentioning is the fact that 38 % of the professionals consulted do not have determined strategic audiences, because they do not work in a segmented manner. They explain that, according to Law 19/2023 of December 9 on transparency, access to public information and good governance, their function is to disseminate any content to all citizens in general. They do not deploy a second segmented layer of information derived from the content. On the other hand, 62 % of institutional referents do try to segment their communication activity by age (44.4 %) or type of group, elderly people, youth, families, businesses or entities and associations (38.9 %), interests (11.1 %) or gender (5.5 %).

When questioned about the logistics of implementing communication programs, more than three-quarters of the sample explained that they have automated their main execution processes through different digital platforms, be it design, account managers, responses, data storage and sending (77.7 %) in order to execute all communication actions with guarantees. However, there is still a significant volume of managers who state that they still do not have optimal automation of the execution processes of PR plans (22.3 %).

Finally, with regard to the evaluation of institutional communication plans, the quantitative and qualitative methodology was questioned at the same stage. Slightly more than half of the professionals say that if they carry out any kind of monitoring, it is informal (52.4 %). Others state that they carry out some kind of qualitative evaluation by taking advantage of citizen contact points such as participation meetings, or through digital monitoring of social networks (14.3 %). Finally, there are communication departments that use neither measurement tools nor indicators (38.1 %).

5.3 Actions and municipal media ecosystem

In relation to the municipal media ecosystem, it can be seen that email (100 %) and WhatsApp (66.7 %) are the most used internally, and the website, social networks and the press service externally (100 %) (Table 6).

External communication involves the use, in addition to the corporate website, with specific spaces for the communication department, and email (100 %), of social networks, especially Facebook (100 %) and Twitter (90.5 %), and those that allow audiovisual, graphic and interactive formats to be articulated, such as YouTube and Instagram (100 %), Flickr (28.6 %), Vimeo (19 %) and Spotify (9.5 %). All departments perform a press office function (100 %) and support or organize events (94.4 %). Other organic channels they manage are the digital newsletter (77.7 %), the municipal magazine (72.2 %), municipal radio (66.6 %), billboards (66.6 %) and municipal street furniture (55.5 %). In addition, in many cases they have an App (61.1 %), Podcasts (38.9 %) and RSS feeds (27.8 %). They also have, in some cases, a corporate WhatsApp (22.2 %) or Telegram (16.7 %).

In addition, 44.4 % of the departments allocate part of their budget to designing and paying for advertising space in local press in print and digital format.

Table 6. Actions and ecosystem of external municipal communication channels

External communication ecosystem	Fa	Fr (%)
Website	18	100
Email	18	100
Social media	18	100
Press service	18	100
Corporate events	17	94.4
Digital newsletter	14	77.7
Municipal magazine	13	72.2
Municipal radio	12	66.6
Municipal billboards	12	66.6
App	11	61.1
Street furniture	10	55.5
Local television	8	44.4
Podcasts	7	38.9
Corporate WhatsApp and/or Telegram	7	38.9
RSS feeds	5	27.8

Source: authors' own.

n = 18 professionals respond (multiple response) about each of the digital channels.

Table 7 shows, on a three-level rating scale (low, medium, high), the reach, impact, level of saturation and personalization, notoriety, consumption of these media by citizens, and the correlation or cost between the efforts of the communication department and the actual reception sought.

Table 7. Rating scale for external municipal communication channels

Outreach	**High (%)**	**Medium (%)**	**Low (%)**
Impact	55.5	44.5	–
Level of saturation	66.6	33.3	–
Level of personalization	61.1	38.9	
Notoriety	27.8	33.3	38.9
Media consumption	66.6	33.3	
Cost	55.5	44.4	–

Source: authors' own.

n = 18 professionals respond to each of the assessments.

6. Discussion and conclusions

The results obtained allow us to answer the three research questions (RQs) linked to the previously established objectives and, in general, are congruent with other similar studies carried out on the management of communication in Spanish local public administrations.

With regard to RQ1, on the structure and hierarchy of communication departments, it is found that the vast majority of Catalan local councils, like their counterparts in other regions of the state, have a global communication office or department (Almansa, 2011; Campillo-Alhama & Martínez-Sala, 2017; Paricio-Esteban & Bruno-Carlos, 2018), having generally moved beyond the structure and functions of the classic press office characteristic of decades ago (Campillo-Alhama, 2011; Cárdenas-Rica, 1998). However, the transition is not complete. We still identify one of the 18 municipalities that calls itself a "press office."

In any case, media relations continue to play a decisive role in municipal communication offices, conceiving the traditional media as the preferred public channel for reaching citizens, as Paricio-Esteban and Bruno-Carlos (2018) pointed out in their study of local councils in the Valencian Community. Likewise, local councils inherit communication models based on punctual and/or improvised actions and there are few or no strategic plans—neither for communication in general, nor for internal communication, nor for crisis communication ...—that help to implement the value of information, its sources and the corporate structures they represent, in line with what has been stated by authors such as García-Gordillo et al. (2021). In general, this work is not systematized, and most of it is reported directly to the Mayor's Office.

The generalized absence of internal communication planning is consistent with previous literature on the object of study, despite it being a fundamental task in any organization (Cuenca & Verazzi, 2020) and most especially in a context of participatory democracy and new public governance, where public employees must participate in decision-making (Ballester-Espinosa, 2019).

In response to RQ2, it is concluded that municipalities' communication plans are not designed following the four-step strategic public relations planning process (research, planning, implementation and evaluation). In this sense, few Barcelona city councils conduct preliminary research, have defined communication objectives, identify their audience map or evaluate their online and offline action plan, in line with the results obtained by Zabala-Cia et al. (2022) in the city councils of another Spanish region, Navarra.

Regarding RQ3, which aimed to elucidate the communication actions and the media ecosystem used by local councils, we observed that, in relation to their internal communication, email is the protagonist in 100 % of cases and WhatsApp in 66.7 %. The fact that mobile instant messaging services such as WhatsApp are essential information and communication tools is a trend that Marcos García et al. (2021) have already pointed out.

On the other hand, the external communication of local councils relies mainly on the following channels: the corporate website—essential for local councils to make the desired content known to potentially mass audiences, as previously noted by authors such as Safai-Amini (2000), Rodríguez et al. (2006) or Rodríguez-Navarro et al. (2017), email and social networks such as Facebook, Twitter, Instagram and YouTube. The two main functions performed by communication departments are press office (100 %) and event support or organization (94.4 %).

The widespread use of digital communication is in line with the private sector (Cuenca-Fontbona et al., 2022). However, the unidirectional use of this type of channel is widespread, obtaining a low rate of feedback from the virtual community and failing to take advantage of its characteristics as a space for participation and dialogue between political representatives and citizens, something already detected by other authors, such as Simelio Solà and Molina-Rodríguez-Navas (2014), Paricio-Esteban et al. (2020), Simelio et al. (2017) or Waters and Williams (2011), among others.

The public sector must be held accountable to society and regain lost trust in public institutions. The absence of a real bidirectionality in municipal communication, added to the conception of communication as mere information to be transmitted—clearly influenced by the prominence of the journalistic training profile of the people responsible for this function—allows us to infer that of the four relational models coined by Grunig and Hunt (1984), for the moment, the first two and oldest predominate: the Press Agent and Public Information, both conceived from the unidirectionality between the organization and its publics. This situation contrasts with a fundamental need and aspiration of public administrations: to seek the development of two-way and dialogic models of institutional communication and public relations that promote citizen participation by facilitating spaces for exchange and attention to their demands (Álvarez-Nobell et al., 2017; Paricio-Esteban et al., 2019). This is the only appropriate way to be accountable to society and to recover the lost trust in public institutions.

In relation to the main hypothesis of the study (H1), the idea that the communication departments of Barcelona's local public administrations of between 10,000 and 20,000 inhabitants contemplate in their praxis the strategic approaches of public relations is refuted. In general, we can affirm that the postulates of Marston (cf. Matilla, 2018) and his RACE model are not yet being applied in the local councils analyzed. The orientation of municipal communication management is eminently tactical, despite the fact that the people responsible for communication admit to being aware of the importance of strategic planning. This incongruence could be justified by the difficulties and limitations intrinsic to this type of institution, ranging from the particular and complex temporal sequence of political-administrative management, to the peculiarities of its hierarchical organization, to the limited availability of human and material resources, or the obligatory dependence of communication on municipal action plans. The imposition of approving and closing budgets prevents the organization of comprehensive communication plans adapted to the needs and urgencies of the moment.

Likewise, as Canel (2018) points out, the confusion between the political and civil service levels has as a consequence "the hypertrophy of the tactical over the strategic." In general, communication strategy remains a function limited to the few trusted appointees of the governing party, while civil servants carry out the technical-tactical tasks (technological management of the network, coverage clippings, etc.).

Probably the main challenge facing local public administrations is to give government communication an apolitical sense, with the aim of building and maintaining mutually beneficial relationships with their publics. As Canel (2018) recommends, it is a matter of placing communication as a cornerstone of the institutional organization chart in a stable and non-fortuitous way, generating at all departmental scales the concept of the essential value of a planned strategy that contributes to the prestige of the public. And as García-Gordillo et al. (2021) propose, communication management should be promoted with a greater role for social networks and a greater capacity for reaction and decision-making by communication departments.

References

Almansa, A. (2011). *Del gabinete de prensa al gabinete de comunicación. La dirección de comunicación en la actualidad*. Comunicación Social Ediciones y Publicaciones.

Álvarez-Nobell, A., Rodríguez, V., & Vadilla, N. (2017). Comunicación digital y accountability social en el seguimiento y la evaluación de la gestión pública de los gobiernos locales en España. *Revista PANGEA*, *8*(1), 1–19. https://doi.org/10.52203/pangea.v8i1.101

Ballester-Espinosa, A. (2019). *La comunicación de las administraciones públicas españolas en el siglo XXI* [Doctoral Thesis]. Universidad de Navarra. https://hdl.handle.net/10171/58866

Bertot, J. C., Jaeger, P. T., & Grimes, J. M. (2010). Using ICTs to create a culture of transparency: E-government and social media as openness and anti-corruption tools for societies. *Government Information Quarterly*, *27*(3), 264–271. https://doi.org/10.1016/j.giq.2010.03.001

Bonsón, E., Royo, S., & Ratkai, M. (2015). Citizens' engagement on local governments' Facebook sites. An empirical analysis: The impact of different media and content types in Western Europe. *Government Information Quarterly*, *32*(1), 52–62. https://doi.org/10.1016/j.giq.2014.11.001

Bonsón, E., Torres, L., Royo, S., & Flores, F. (2012). Local e-government 2.0: Social media and corporate transparency in municipalities. *Government Information Quarterly*, *29*(2), 123–132. https://doi.org/10.1016/j.giq.2011.10.001

Campillo-Alhama, C., (2011). *Comunicación pública y gestión estratégica municipal. Un estudio exploratorio sobre la agenda temática*. Tirant lo Blanch

Campillo-Alhama, C., & Martínez-Sala, A. M. (2017). Comunicación integrada 2.0 en la Administración Municipal. *El Profesional de la Información*, *26*(3), 507–515. https://doi.org/10.3145/epi.2017.may.17

Canel, M. J. (2018). *La Comunicación de la Administración Pública. Para gobernar con vla sociedad*. Fondo de Cultura Económica.

Canel, M. J., & Luoma-aho, V. (2017). *Public sector communication: Closing gaps between citizen and public organizations*. Wiley-Blackwell.

Cárdenas-Rica, M. L. (1998). Profesionalización de los gabinetes de prensa. *Ámbitos. Revista Internacional de Comunicación*, 1, 131-141.

Castillo-Esparcia, A., Moreno, Á., & Capriotti-Peri, P. (2020). Relaciones públicas y comunicación institucional ante la crisis del COVID-19. *Revista Internacional de Relaciones Públicas, 19*(10), 1–6. http://dx.doi.org/10.5783/RIRP-19-2020-01-01-06

Corbetta, P. (2003). *Metodologías y técnicas de investigación social*. McGraw-Hill.

Compte-Pujol, M. (2016). Revisión y clasificación de los paradigmas científicos de las relaciones públicas del siglo XXI. *Opción: Revista de ciencias humanas y sociales, 9*, 371–386. http://www.redalyc.org/articulo.oa?id=31048482020

Criado, J. I., & Villodre, J. (2020). Delivering public services through social media in European local governments. An interpretative framework using semantic algorithms. *Local Government Studies, 47*(2), 253–275. https://doi.org/10.1080/03003930.2020.1729750

Cuenca, J. (2018). *Como hacer un plan de Comunicación. La investigación preliminar*. Colección Dircom-UOC.

Cuenca, J., & Verazzi, L. (2020). *Comunicación Interna Total*. Colección Dircom-UOC.

Cuenca-Fontbona, J., & Puentes-Rivera, I. (2019). Relaciones Públicas avanzadas: Confianza. *Trípodos, 45*, 7–12. https://doi.org/10.51698/tripodos.2019.45

Cuenca-Fontbona, J., Compte-Pujol, M., & Zeler, I. (2022). The strategy applied to Public Relations in the digital environment: The Spanish case. *Revista Latina de Comunicación Social, 80*, 163–182. https://doi.org/10.4185/RLCS-2022-1537

Cutlip, S. M., Center, A. H., & Broom, G. M. (2012). *Effective public relations* (11th ed.). Prentice Hall.

Dozier, D. M., Grunig, L. A., & Grunig, J. E. (1995). *Managers guide to excellence in public relations and communication management*. Lawrence Erlbaum Associates.

Espino González, J. (2022). La comunicación institucional en la crisis de la COVID-19: El caso del ayuntamiento de Málaga. *Revista de Comunicación de la SEECI, 55*, 67–92. https://doi.org/10.15198/seeci.2022.55.e774

Falkheimer, J., & Heide, M. (2018). *Strategic communication. An introduction*. Routledge.

García-Gordillo, M., & Pérez-Curiel, C. (2021). *Comunicación institucional pública: retos y realidades*. UOC.

Gértrudix, M., Gertrudis-Casado, M.C., & Álvarez-García, S. (2016). Consumption of public institutions' open data by Spanish citizens. *El profesional de la información, 25*(4), 535–544. https://doi.org/10.3145/epi.2016.jul.03

Gillham, B. (2005). *Research interviewing. The range of techniques*. Open University Press.

Graham, M., & Avery, E. J. (2013). Government public relations and social media: An analysis of the perceptions and trends of social media use at the local government level. *Public Relations Journal, 7*(4), 1–21. https://prjournal.instituteforpr.org/wp-content/uploads/2013GrahamAvery.pdf

Grunig, J. E. (1992). *Excellence in PR and communication management*. Lawrence Erlbaum Associates.

Grunig, J. E., & Hunt, T. (1984). *Managing public relations*. Holt, Rinehart and Winston.

Guillamón, M. D., Ríos, A. M., Gesuele, B., & Metallo, C. (2016). Factors influencing social media use in local governments: The case of Italy and Spain. *Government Information Quarterly, 33*(3), 460–417. https://doi.org/10.1016/j.giq.2016.06.005

Kim, S., & Lee, J. (2012). E-Participation, transparency, and trust in local government. *Public Administration Review, 72*(6), 819–828. https://doi.org/10.1111/j.1540-6210.2012.02593.x

Kinnear, S. (2022). Las relaciones públicas en el sector público. In A. Theaker (Ed.), *El Manual de Comunicación y Relaciones Públicas* (6th ed., pp. 421–442). Profit.

Krippendorf, K. (1990). *Metodología del análisis de contenido*. Paidós.

Landeta, J. (2006). Current validity of the Delphi method in social sciences. *Technological Forecasting and Social Change, 73*(5), 467–482. https://doi.org/10.1016/j.techfore.2005.09.002

Law 19/2014, de 9 de Diciembre, de Transparencia, Acceso a la Información Pública y Buen Gobierno. Jefatura del Estado (2013). Boletín Oficial del Estado, 295, de 10/12/2013. 97.922 a 97.952. Accessed May 10, 2023, from https://www.boe.es/eli/es/l/2013/12/09/19/con

Law 19/2014, de 29 de Diciembre, de Transparencia, Acceso a la Información Pública y Buen Gobierno. Comunidad Autónoma de Cataluña (2015). Boletín Oficial del Estado, 18, de 21/01/2015. 4.300 a 4.342. Accessed May 10, 2023, from https://bit.ly/3j1Dgh2

Lev-On, A., & Steinfeld, N. (2015). Local engagement online: Municipal Facebook pages as hubs of interaction. *Government Information Quarterly*, *32*(3), 299–307. https://doi.org/10.1016/j.giq.2015.05.007

Lichtman, M. (2006). *Qualitative research in education. A user's guide*. Sage.

Loópez-Aranguren, E. (1989). El análisis de contenido. In M. García Ferrando, J. Ibáñez y F. Alvira (Comp.), *El análisis de la realidad social. Métodos y técnicas de investigación* (2nd ed., 383–414). Alianza.

Manfredi-Sánchez, J. L., Corcoy-Rius, M., & Herranz-de-la-Casa, J. (2017). Breaking news? Journalistic criteria in the publication of news on Spanish municipal websites (2011–2016). *El profesional de la información*, *26*(3), 412–420. https://doi.org/10.3145/epi.2017.may.07

Marcos García, S., Doménech-Fabregat, H., & Casero-Ripollés, A. (2021). The platformization of institutional political communication. The use of WhatsApp by local administrators. *Revista Latina de Comunicación Social*, *79*, 100–125. https://www.doi.org/10.4185/RLCS-2021-1520

Matilla, K. (2018). *Cómo hacer un plan estratégico de comunicación. Volumen I: Un modelo de planificación estratégica, paso a paso*. UOC.

Molina-Rodríguez-Navas, P. M., Medranda Morales, N., & Muñoz Lalinde, J. (2021). Transparency for participation through the communication approach. *International Journal of Geo-Information*, *10*, 586. https://doi.org/10.3390/ijgi10090586

Molina-Rodríguez-Navas, P. M., Rodríguez Breijo, V., Corcoy Rius, M., & Vadillo Bengoa, N. (2017). La transparencia de los ayuntamientos de Cataluña antes de la entrada en vigor de la legislación estatal y autonómica. *Anales de Documentación*, *20*(2). http://dx.doi.org/10.6018/analesdoc.20.2.288151

Moon, M. J. (2002). The evolution of e-government among municipalities: Rhetoric or reality? *Public Administration Review*, *62*(4), 424–433. https://doi.org/10.1111/0033-3352.00196

Moreno Sardà, A., Molina-Rodríguez-Navas, P. M., & Corcoy Rius, M. (2013). The information published by local governments. The websites of Catalonia's municipal governments. *Revista Latina de Comunicación Social*, *68*, 502–528. https://doi.org/10.4185/RLCS-2013-987

Ohme, J. (2018). Updating citizenship? The effects of digital media use on citizenship understanding and political participation. *Information, Communication & Society*, *22*(13), 1903–1928. https://doi.org/10.1080/1369118X.2018.1469657

Oliveira, A. (2018). *Como hacer un plan de Comunicación. Volumen II: Públicos y Stakeholders*. Colección Dircom-UOC.

Paricio, M. P., Bruno-Carlos, T., & Aznar, H. (2019). Modelos bidireccionales de relaciones públicas y comunicación municipal. Análisis de los portales de transparencia y participación ciudadana en los ayuntamientos de más de 10.000 habitantes de la Comunidad Valenciana. *Trípodos*, *45*, 89–110. https://www.raco.cat/index.php/Tripodos/article/view/363335/457702

Paricio-Esteban, M. P., & Bruno-Carlos, T. (2018). La gestión de las relaciones con los medios en los gabinetes de comunicación de los ayuntamientos valencianos. *Communication Papers*, *7*(15), 213–229. https://raco.cat/index.php/communication/article/view/346945

Paricio-Esteban, P., Bruno-Carlos, T., Alonso-Romero, E., & García-Alcober, M. P. (2020). Transparency and citizen participation web pages and portals for managing public relations with local stakeholders. *Profesional de la información*, *29*(3). https://doi.org/10.3145/epi.2020.may.35

Reddick, C. G., Chatfield, A. T., & Ojo, A. (2017). A social media text analytics framework for double-loop learning for citizen-centric public services: A case study of a local government Facebook use. *Government Information Quarterly*, *34*(1), 110–125. https://doi.org/10.1016/j.giq.2016.11.001

Rodrich Portugal, R. (2012). Fundamentos de la Comunicación Institucional: una aproximación histórica y conceptual de la profesión. *Revista de Comunicación*, *11*, 212–234. https://revistadecomunicacion.com/article/view/2763

Rodríguez, M. M., Marauri Castillo, I., & Pérez, J. A. (2006). La comunicación institucional y de servicios. Las páginas web municipales de las capitales de provincia españolas. *Anàlisi*, *33*, 63–78. https://raco.cat/index.php/Analisi/article/view/51740

Rodríguez-Breijo, V., Simelio, N., & Molina-Rodríguez-Navas, P. (2021). Council Press offices as sources of political information: Between journalism for accountability and propaganda. *Future Internet*, *13*(2), 34. https://doi.org/10.3390/fi13020034

Safai-Amini, M. (2000). Information technologies: Challenge and opportunities for local governments. *Journal of Government Information*, *27*(4), 471–479.

Schmidthuber, L., Ingrams, A., & Hilgers, D. (2020). Government openness and public trust: The mediating role of democratic capacity. *Public Administration Review*, *81*(1), 91–109. https://doi.org/10.1111/puar.13298

Shaw, I. (2003). *La evaluación cualitativa. Introducción a los métodos cualitativos*. Paidós.

Silverman, D. (2006). *Interpreting qualitative data* (3rd ed.). Sage.

Simelio, N., Ginesta, X., de San Eugenio Vela, J., & Corcoy, M. (2017). Journalism, transparency and citizen participation: A methodological tool to evaluate information published on municipal websites. *Information, Communication & Society*, *22*(3), 369–385. https://doi.org/10.1080/1369118X.2017.1386706

Simelio Solà, N., & Molina-Rodríguez-Navas, P. M. (2014). Comunicación pública y participación ciudadana. El uso de Twitter en los ayuntamientos de Cataluña. *Historia y Comunicación Social*, *19*, 479–490. http://dx.doi.org/10.5209/rev_HICS.2014.v19.45043

Solito, L., & Materassi, L. (2020). On a municipality-wide scale. Social media use in Italian municipalities: Information and interaction. *AdComunica*, *20*, 151–172. https://doi.org/10.6035/2174-0992.2020.20.7

Thorson, K., Medeiros, M., Cotter, K., Chen, Y., Rodgers, K., Bae, A., & Baykaldi, S. (2020). Platform civics: Facebook in the local information infrastructure. *Digital Journalism*, *8*(10), 1231–1257. https://doi.org/10.1080/21670811.2020.1842776

Tolbert, C. J., & Mossberger, K. (2006). The effects of e-government on trust and confidence in government. *Public Administration Review*, *66*(3), 354–369. https://doi.org/10.1111/j.1540-6210.2006.00594.x

Waters, R. D., & Williams, J. M. (2011). Squawking, tweeting, cooing, and hooting: Analyzing the communication patterns of government agencies on Twitter. *Journal of Public Affairs*, *11*(4), 353–363. https://doi.org/10.1002/pa.385

Wilcox, D. L., Cameron, G. T., & Reber, B. H. (2015). *Public relations. Strategies and tactics*. (Global ed.). Pearson Education.

Xifra, J. (2014). *Manual de relaciones públicas e institucionales*. Tecnos.

Zabala-Cia, O., Lorenzo-Sola, F., & González-Pacanowski, T. (2022). Interactividad en redes sociales para crear relaciones de confianza: Ayuntamientos de Navarra en tránsito. *Revista de Ciencias de la Comunicación e Información*, *27*, 25–44. https://doi.org/10.35742/rcci.2022.27.e246

Zerfass, A., Verčič, D., Verhoeven, P., Moreno, A., & Tench, R. (2019). *European Communication Monitor 2019. Exploring trust in the profession, transparency, artificial intelligence and new content strategies. Results of a survey in 46 countries*. EACD/EUPRERA, Quadriga Media Berlin. https://www.communicationmonitor.eu/2019/05/23/ecm-european-communication-monitor-2019/

Mariola Tàrrega Moltó, Jordi de San Eugenio Vela, and
Xavier Ginesta Portet

Defining the challenges of territorial branding and its implementation: A network approach

Abstract: The discipline of place branding has been conceptualized, generally, from a normative perspective that does not include evidence emerging from professional practices in the field. For this reason, among others, the public relations discipline has been absent from the multidisciplinary field of place branding. Nonetheless, this paper demonstrates that the role of public relations is central place branding. This conclusion emerges after analyzing the most relevant studies in the field from a theoretical-practice perspective and incorporating the empirical results from eight consultancy projects carried out by the research team TRACTE from Uvic-UCC. Public relations is key to conceptualize trustworthy, committed and mutually engaging relationships between the different stakeholders involved in place branding projects. Communication becomes essential to conceptualize, design and implement place brands from a bottom-up perspective that engages with the publics and transforms citizens into brand ambassadors.

Keywords: stakeholders, place branding, political power, communication, public relations, trust, commitment

1. Introduction

Place branding has been defined as a new way of imagining the territory, a hybrid process of managing and continuously improving its image (Lucarelli, 2018). This integrative vision defined by Lucarelli (2018) and Jiménez Morales and San Eugenio (2011), among others, refers to a hybrid sociopolitical process that combines stakeholder management, coordination with a set of public policies, and communication. This definition of place branding differs from previous ones, more reductionist conceptions, where the focus was on tourism promotion and economic opportunities.

Historically, place branding had been approached through techniques applied in the corporate field that were mimetically implemented in defining the place (Compte-Pujol et al., 2016; San Eugenio, 2011). However, this is problematic. Understanding and managing a complex identity is essential in the management of territorial brands. The brand is not only a device for promoting the place but also a mechanism for managing the identities of its citizens in a complex, *glocal* environment (San Eugenio, 2011; San Eugenio, Ginesta, & Kavaratzis, 2019). Therefore, it is essential that new approaches to place branding incorporate elements to understand the sociopolitical and geographical reality of the place (Govers & Go, 2009).

The objective of this chapter is to understand the factors that determine the success of place branding projects and the role that communication, understood from the perspective of Public Relations, plays in them. Our starting hypothesis is that a detailed analysis of the factors that determine the success of a place branding strategy also highlights the central role of Communication, specifically those aspects related to the discipline of Public Relations.

2. Theoretical framework: Communication and public relations in the context of place branding

One of the main objectives of place branding is the strategic positioning of a territory to attract tourists, talent, and investments from international markets (Anholt, 2007; Fernández-Cavia, 2011; Lopez-Lita & Benlloch, 2005; Papadopoulos, 2004; Skinner, 2021; Swain et al., 2023). Therefore, place branding plays a key role in public diplomacy strategies (Moilanen & Rainisto, 2009) and to the projection of non-stereotypical images of the place (Piñeiro-Naval & Igartua Perosanz, 2012). Nonetheless, one of the problems in the field of place branding, as highlighted by Vuigner (2017), is the lack of conceptual clarity, lack of solid empirical evidence, and lack of interest in studying the political and institutional dimensions of place branding. It is a field where normative conceptions about what place branding should contribute and accomplish abound (Skinner, 2021), but it is much more difficult to find theorization based on empirical evidence obtained from social research.

Thus, place branding is a hybrid and integrative discipline (Jiménez Morales & San Eugenio, 2011; Lucarelli, 2018). Defining a territorial brand is a hybrid sociopolitical process in which citizens, economic agents, digital communities, media actors, spatial planners, and policymakers work in a relational and interactive manner (Lucarelli, 2018). This approach diverges from previous reductionist views of place branding, where the process was limited to tourism and economic purposes. This multidimensional and relational approach emphasizes how managing relationships between different stakeholders form or influence the successful implementation of a territorial brand (Compte-Pujol et al., 2018).

Both Fernández-Cavia and Huertas (2014) and Robson (2021) highlight that place branding studies have ignored or not considered the role that a discipline like Public Relations can contribute to a conception of place branding beyond tourism promotion. Also, within normative conceptions of what place branding should contribute and accomplish, the role of communication or public relations is important but often not explicitly presented as such. For instance, the idea of moving away from simplistic promotional approaches was also defended by Anholt (2009), even though he never used the term 'public relations.' He argued that the image associated with a place must be complex, desirable, and multifaceted. To reach this desirable outcome, it is necessary to move away from commercial campaigns that simplify the image of specific products or services and instead aim for cultural excellence (Anholt, 2009). In a similar line, latest studies on the relationship between place branding and spatial planning also highlight the need to create place narratives that contribute to the improvement of socio-spatial and spatial/economic conditions of a place (Van Assche et al., 2020). Nonetheless, most communication activities within place branding literature are only considered as a mean to an end, touristic promotion.

Communication is not regarded by most place branding scholars as the central element in managing relationships among stakeholders, which are key in policy design and identity creation. Latest studies in the field use terms such as 'destination marketing' (Swain et al., 2023), 'place marketing' (Skinner, 2021) or 'broadcasting activities' (Ma et al., 2019). The choice of terms is not neutral in these cases. Swain et al. (2023) advocate for the use of persuasion theory in place branding research but only to study how information provided by marketing campaigns influences tourists' attitudes toward a destination and they highlight the need to use storytelling in promotion activities. In the same line, Ma et al.'s (2019) systematic review use the term 'broadcasting activities' to refer to a three-stage role of communication within place branding processes based on first, promotion; then marketing; and finally corporate branding. In these approaches, communication does not play a role in building relationships with key stakeholders in early stages of brand building such as in citizen/stakeholder participation processes.

Researchers studying citizen participation processes emphasize the importance of power relationships to ensure the success of local initiatives, such as participatory budgeting (Escobar, 2017; Berry et al., 2019; Sintomer et al., 2008). To counterbalance power imbalances between a public administration with the ability to make public policies and citizens with limited voice, some academics point to the need to define citizen participation processes that clearly define the decision-making power granted to each party, shared resources for decision-making, and responsibility in decision-making (Elliott et al., 2019).

Kemp et al. (2012) highlight the importance of citizen/stakeholder participation to legitimize the place branding project during its implementation phase.

Public relations theory, particularly critical public relations theory (L'Etang & Pieczka, 2006), offers a way to overcome the limitations of current approaches to the role of communication in place branding studies and to integrate the evidence highlighted by citizen participation literature. Within the discipline of Public Relations, there has been much debate about one of the key elements of place branding: the role of communication in relationships between organizations, their audiences, and stakeholders (Bruning & Ledingham, 1999; Cutlip & Broom, 1999; Edwards, 2018; L'Etang & Pieczka, 2006; Theunissen & Wan Noordin, 2012). Based on a normative and ideal conceptualization of relationships between stakeholders and organizations, Grunig (1992) spoke of the need to create symmetrical and mutually satisfying relationships, emphasizing the central role of communication in this process. Grunig (1992) proposed that relationships with stakeholders should be based on trust, mutual control, satisfaction, and commitment. This symmetrical conception of relationships with stakeholders has been subsequently questioned and nuanced by scholars adopting the perspective of critical Public Relations (L'Etang & Pieczka, 2006; Piezcka, 2015; Theunissen & Wan Noordin, 2012). There is no symmetry between an organization and the stakeholders with whom it relates and involves; power relationships are always present and determine the influence capacity of one over the other (L'Etang et al., 2012).

The public relations critical and non-normative conception of relationships with stakeholders is useful for designing and implementing stakeholder participation processes in place branding, as pointed out by authors like Kavaratzis and Kalandides (2015) and San Eugenio, Ginesta, and Kavaratzis (2019). In that sense, to avoid limiting the role of communication strategies in place branding to a single promotional action, the concept needs to be understood as a hybrid process (San Eugenio, 2011). When place branding is conceptualized as a hybrid process, the role of communication strategies is not limited to a single promotional action (San Eugenio, 2011).

3. Methodology

This chapter reviews, from a Public Relations perspective, the results of empirical studies conducted by the Audiovisual Translation, Communication and Territory (TRACTE) research group at Uvic-UCC on eight place branding projects carried out between 2013 and 2023.

The review of the empirical studies is based on the analysis of two dimensions:

- Factors that determine the design, implementation and development of place branding.
- Power relations among spheres of action.

The aim of the analysis is to identify the potential role of public relations in aiding success and failure elements in each of the dimensions. The analyzed projects are listed in Tables 1 and 2.

Table 1. List of place branding projects coordinated and elaborated by the research group TRACTE, uVic-UCC between 2013 and 2023

Project	Contractor/funder	Brand logo
Tourism Development Project "Boscos de bruixes i bandolers"	Association of Municipalities Boscos de Bruixes	*Fig 1. Forests of Witches and Bandits*
Design and conceptualization of the brand "Vic"	Vic City Council	*Fig 2. Vic, a city tailored to human scale*
Design and conceptualization of the brand "Empordà"	Figueres City Council, Alt Empordà County Council, and Baix Empordà County Council	*Fig 3. Empordà, touched by the gods*
Design and conceptualization of the brand "Pla de l'Estany"	Pla de l'Estany County Council	*Fig 4. Pla de l'Estany, the county that beats*
Design and conceptualization of the brand "El Vendrell"	El Vendrell City Council	*Fig 5. El Vendrell, loves you!*
Design and conceptualization of the brand "Espai Agrari de la Baixa Tordera"	Barcelona Provincial Council	*Fig 6. Agrarian Space, Baixa Tordera*

(*continued*)

Table 1. Continued

Project	Contractor/funder	Brand logo
Review of the brand plan for the city of Manlleu	Manlleu City Council	*Fig 7. Manlleu, Ter's capital*
Design and conceptualization of the brand "Masquefa"	Masquefa City Council, Barcelona Provincial Council	*Fig 8. Masquefa's connects*

Table 2. List of municipalities and/or regions involved in the analyzed place branding projects

Projects	Municipalities and/or regions involved
Tourism Development Project "Boscos de bruixes i bandolers"	Arbúcies, Viladrau, Sant Hilari Sacalm, Sant Feliu Sasserra, Olost
Design and conceptualization of the brand "Vic"	Vic
Design and conceptualization of the brand "Empordà"	Municipios del Alt y Baix Empordà
Design and conceptualization of the brand "Pla de l'Estany"	Municipios del Pla de l'Estany
Design and conceptualization of the brand "El Vendrell"	El Vendrell
Design and conceptualization of the brand "Espai Agrari de la Baixa Tordera"	Palafolls, Blanes, Todera, Malgrat de Mar, Santa Susana.
Review of the brand plan for the city of Manlleu	Manlleu
Design and conceptualization of the brand "Masquefa"	Masquefa

The aforementioned projects use applied social research methods particularly, methodological triangulation involving in-depth interviews, focus group discussions, and open online surveys for citizens. The development of these projects involved the coexistence of a theoretical-practical perspective, allowing researchers to offer place branding consulting services to the Public Administration and, once the project is completed, transform this consultancy into a publishable scientific study in internationally impactful journals. Notable among these projects are the works of San Eugenio et al. (2019), as well as those of San Eugenio, Ginesta, and Kavaratzis (2019), Ginesta et al. (2020), or San Eugenio et al. (2023). Additionally, to complete the circle of the three basic pillars of the university's impact on society (research, teaching, and transfer), these works have contributed to the development of the core curriculum of the Postgraduate Program in Place Branding and Strategic Territory Management offered by the Uvic-UCC Graduate School.

4. Results

4.1 The role of communication or public relations in the factors that determine the implementation and development of place branding

With clear political, economic, and participatory implications, Public Administrations that develop territorial brands face complex implementation challenges. A detailed analysis of the factors that determine the success of place branding strategies also highlights the central role of communication, understood from the perspective of Public Relations.

The development and implementation of the projects presented in the methodology of this research can be divided into three phases (Ginesta et al., 2020; San Eugenio, Ginesta, & Kavaratzis, 2019; San Eugenio et al., 2019; San Eugenio et al., 2023). The first phase involves conceptualization and fieldwork aimed at understanding the demographic and socioeconomic composition of the place under study. This initial phase includes the development of a SWOT analysis based on existing technical documentation, as well as the deployment of applied social research using qualitative techniques (focus groups and in-depth interviews) and quantitative methods (surveys). The second phase is the brand design phase, which involves the preparation of an executive brief by the research team, based on the social research results, and made available to the communication agency responsible for developing the final graphics and slogan of the brand. The third phase is the brand's legitimization, which involves the contracting party developing a communication plan that will be used to implement the brand and transform citizens into its civilian ambassadors.

In the conceptualization phase, the need to deeply understand the sociopolitical and geographical reality of the place (Govers & Go, 2009) is crucial. Anholt (2007) even emphasizes considering elements such as the nature of the perception of reality, social cohesion, and the socio-cultural identity of the place. Thus, Ginesta and San Eugenio (2020) argue that the use of social research techniques is key to understanding an existing image that is complex, must be incorporated into the project, and will be crucial for the success of the citizen participation processes involved in place branding. As L'Etang and Pieczka (2006) highlight, prior social research is already part of Public Relations since its functions include environmental analysis, analysis of issues of interest, and situation analysis, among others.

In the deployment of social research, it is understood that the key to success lies in adopting a bottom-up strategy (Anholt, 2007) where there is key participation from all local stakeholders (San Eugenio, Ginesta, & Kavaratzis, 2019). At this point, it is understood that a communication strategy focused solely on promotion and not on supporting this bottom-up process is a barrier to success (San Eugenio, Ginesta, & Kavaratzis, 2019). As highlighted by Robson (2021), emphasizing a fruitful relationship and the participation of various stakeholders, including citizens, is an opportunity to use public relations tools in place branding strategies. Participation in key decision-making by citizens and stakeholders prevents brands from being reduced to mere empty logos and slogans (San Eugenio, Ginesta, & Kavaratzis, 2019). In turn, participation provides the project with legitimacy during its implementation phase (Kavaratzis & Kalanides, 2015) and civic awareness (Kemp et al., 2012).

From the beginning of the process, in order to seek the complicity of residents, Ginesta and San Eugenio (2020) emphasize the essential role of communication. Communication must be established at three levels: (a) communicating to educate and explain the project, (b) communicating to set expectations and maintain positive tension about the project, (c) communicating to promote constant citizen participation. They attribute to communication a role that goes beyond promotion and becomes a key element of citizen participation, as well as the legitimization and success of the project. Increased interaction between residents and political agents helps the public administration legitimize its narrative and implement a multi-level branding process in the future (Ginesta & San Eugenio, 2020).

From a stakeholder management approach, San Eugenio, Ginesta, and Kavaratzis (2019) contribute a new role to the traditional function of Public Relations: the relationship with the media. Based on the project that created the regional brand in North-Catalonia, "Empordà, tocal pels deus" (Table 1) [Empordà, touch by gods], these authors emphasize the need to incorporate local media as key stakeholders to promote necessary public debates throughout the process of legitimizing the new brand. Local media are not only a promotional tool but also essential for creating a link with local public policies (San Eugenio, Ginesta, & Kavaratzis, 2019). This strong relationship between local media and the public administration was also important to implement most of the brands informed in Table 1, especially in the municipalities of Vic, Manlleu and Masquefa, as well as in the county of Pla de l'Estany.

The excellence in public relations advocated by Grunig (1992) speaks of stakeholder relationships that should be built on the foundations of trust and mutual control, satisfaction, and commitment. In this sense, the brand design phase cannot be carried out without these theoretical foundations. The complicity between the social research team and the communication agency, with the public administration acting as a mediator, is essential for a brand to be successfully developed. The municipalities of Vic and Masquefa have been able to implement city brands that have successfully surpass different electoral periods, due to the establishment of coordination mechanisms among the stakeholders involved in the conceptualization and implementation process (Ginesta et al., 2020). On the contrary, the city of El Vendrell adapted the city brand to specific touristic purposes after the 2019 local elections in Spain. Therefore, several factors can break the triangle among the social research team, the communication agency and the public administration, allowing us to support those authors who, from the field of Public Relations, have criticized Grunig's normative positions (1992): the alteration of the composition of the municipal council due to municipal elections or a government crisis that breaks the necessary relationship between the research team and the agency, the elongation of time between the conceptualization phase and the design phase, or simply the always turbulent human relationships where egos prevail over cooperation. Consequently, understanding the power relationships (L'Etang & Pieczka, 2006; Theunissen & Wan Noordin, 2012) that exist among the participating actors in the conceptualization and design process of a place brand is important for preventing long-term crises.

Finally, in the legitimization and implementation phase, Ginesta and San Eugenio (2020) state that one of the success factors of a place branding project is for the brand to be part of urban policies and place sustainability. In this regard, San Eugenio, Ginesta, and Kavaratzis (2019), analyzing the conceptualization and implementation process of the brand "Empordà, touch by the gods," argue that without the complicity of all stakeholders, the necessary link between place branding strategy and other public policies it may affect cannot be achieved. For instance, in the project Masquefa, the brand plan was designed in coordination with the local urban agenda facilitating the implementation of the project.

Specifically, to maintain trusting and complicit relationships between the involved agents, San Eugenio, Ginesta, and Kavaratzis (2019) propose that public administrations create municipal brand councils where the long-term participation of both public and private stakeholders can be maintained in the review of place brand objectives. Consequently, brand councils become spaces where power relationships among stakeholders are shaped to evolve toward relationships built on trust and mutual control. However, not all the projects developed by the research team finished with the creation of some mechanisms of coordination. At the end, this depends on the leadership of the public administration and how it wants to shape the local storytelling in the long term. For example, the conceptualization of the brand Manlleu has been done in parallel of the definition of a communication plan and a new organizational chart processes map that contribute to give coherence to all the actions linked with the brand.

4.2 Space for success in place branding: Power relations among spheres of action

Based on the empirical evidence gathered, one of the most important elements to a successful place branding project is the interaction among three spheres of action: the political system in place, the media system and other communication agents (design agencies, for example), as well as the socioeconomic stakeholders. The interaction among those three spheres needs to be understood, defined, and planned in advance taking into consideration existing power imbalances and dynamics specifics to each context.

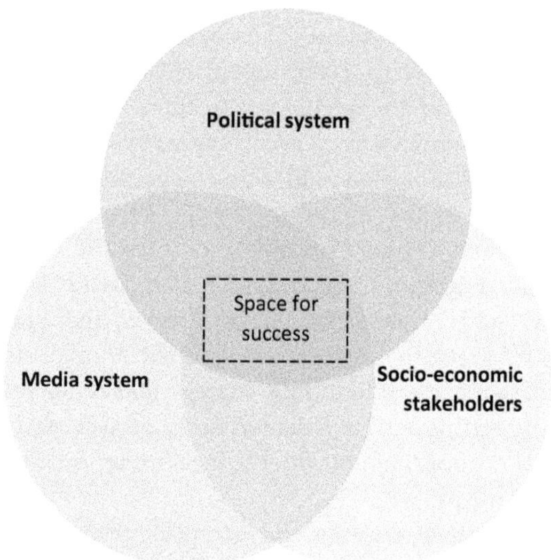

Figure 1. Spheres of action and space for success in place branding.
Source: authors' own.

To understand the role of Public Relations in place branding, we step out of functionalist perspectives of Public Relations. Public Relations is understood as a continuum and a flow of purposive communication, rather than a managerial function (Edwards & Hodge, 2011).

The conceptualization stage

The role of Public Relations in the development of place branding projects is key throughout the development of a place branding project, but it plays a special role in the initial conceptualization stage of the process. Based on the empirical results of our analysis, there are two success elements in the conceptualization stage of place branding projects: the use of social research methods to understand the sociopolitical context and the integration of citizen/stakeholder participation processes. In that sense, mapping the locus of decision-making power and the role of each stakeholder in the decision-making process of each stage in the project is essential.

Using a critical public relations perspective and stepping out of the idea that stakeholder relationships need to be operationalized from a symmetrical perspective (Edwards, 2018) will help unpacking the power relationship dynamics between the different stakeholders. For instance, acknowledging power imbalance between local government and civic society organizations involved in the project, local authorities will always have the final saying on the final shaping of the project, might help set up initial expectations and final outcomes of the project. In each context, the intersection between different power dynamics and diversity of stakeholders will influence the final map of power dynamics.

The design phase

The empirical evidence indicates that the management of the relationship with the creative agency in charge of the design of the brand is key. To that point, the communication dynamics between the management of the project and the agency needs to be understood as not just a unilateral exercise but as a dialogical process that will eventually shape the final outcome, the brand. This dialogical process is not an equal-to-equal exchange (Piezcka, 2015). The project leaders hold the essential knowledge that needs to be used in the creation of the new brand (derived from the participation processes and social scanning of the context). This knowledge needs to be effectively communicated to the agency. In return, the agency needs to effectively communicate its needs (timing, in-house expertise, terms and conditions).

Legitimation and implementation

Integrating the project into the design of urban policies and having a fully developed communications plan are the two key success elements in this final stage. Anholt (2007) strongly criticized merely promotional approaches to communicating place branding projects. From a critical Public Relations perspective, the communication plan needs to acknowledge that communicating the outcome of the project will shape and influence the socio-cultural context where the project takes place (Edwards, 2018).

However, the legitimation process of a new place brand starts before its design and implementation. During the conceptualizing phase, political and media systems must work together in order to strengthen the need to create this new place brand and the benefits it will give to the territory. Without the collaboration of the media system is impossible that political actors can situate the need of a new place brand in the collective imaginary of the citizens. Taking into consideration that, depending the context, political and media actors cooperate and compete at the same time, the development of a place brand allow them to find a new space for cooperation in benefit of the citizens of a territory.

5. Final remarks

Public Relations, as a communication discipline focused on stakeholder relationships, can play a key role in articulating the relationship between the three spheres of action in place branding projects (political system, media system and socioeconomic stakeholders). The review of eight projects of place branding (San Eugenio, Ginesta, & Kavaratzis, 2019; San Eugenio et al., 2019; San Eugenio et al., 2023; Ginesta et al., 2020) indicates that the shared space between the three spheres of action, which can be articulated through participation processes, is key to the success of the project (see Figure 1). The evidence points out to higher success stories when the communication between the three spheres is strategic, fluid and articulated considering the different power imbalances between each of them (L'Etang, 2012). From these three spheres of action perspective, communication activities or in this case, public relations, is not only needed in the promotional activities of the brand during the implementation phase.

In conclusion, despite the normative connotation of the place branding discipline, communication, understood from the field of Public Relations, plays a central role in the success of conceptualization, design, and implementation projects of place brands. While reference authors in the field of Public Relations, such as Fernández-Cavia and Huertas (2014) or Robson (2021), criticize the limited impact of Public Relations in the theoretical framework of place branding, it can be affirmed that the success of place branding campaigns would not be possible without considering Public Relations in the center of the process. However, although a normative view of Public Relations suggests considering trust and complicity among the involved stakeholders as the key to success in a place branding campaign, evidence from our research shows that imbalance power-relations among the actors involved in a place branding strategy have to be considered when we search spaces for cooperation. Power relations, and how these are managed in each different context and territory, draw the final space for success in a place branding campaign (see Figure 1). Hence, Public Relations become essential during all the conceptualization, design and implementation process of a place brand, due to they give the tools in order to manage complex, competitive and cooperative relationships among the stakeholders involved.

This is evident from the analysis of the empirical results of the eight place branding projects developed by the TRACTE research group at Uvic-UCC between 2013 and 2023 (San Eugenio, Ginesta, & Kavaratzis, 2019; San Eugenio et al., 2019; San Eugenio et al., 2023; Ginesta et al., 2020). Their results point to a central role of Public Relations actions in the success of these projects. This role is not solely focused on the promotion phase of the initiative but also plays a key role in managing citizen participation and stakeholders, and therefore in the political and social legitimization of the project.

References

Anholt, S. (2007). *Competitive identity: The new brand management for nations, cities and regions.* Palgrave Macmillan.

Anholt, S. (2009). Introductory essay: Why national image matters. In World Tourism Organization (Ed.), *Handbook on tourism destination branding* (pp. 9–16). World Tourism Organization.

Berry, L. H., Koski, J., Verkuijl, C., Strambo, C., & Piggot, G. (2019). *Making space: How public participation shapes environmental decision-making.* Stockholm Environment Institute.

Bruning, S., & Ledingham, J. (1999). Relationships between organizations and publics: Development of a multi-dimensional organization–public relationship Scale. *Public Relations Review*, *25*, 157–170.

Compte-Pujol, M., De Urquijo, B., & Matilla, K. (2016). La investigación en marcas de territorio y diplomacia pública en España. Un estudio bibliométrico de las revistas científicas españolas especializadas en Comunicación indexadas en Latindex (1980–2016). *Anales de Documentación, 19*(2), 1–53.

Compte-Pujol, M., San Eugenio-Vela, J., & Frigola-Reig, J. (2018). Key elements in defining Barcelona's place values: The contribution of residents' perceptions from an internal place branding perspective. *Place Brand Public Diplomacy, 14*, 245–259.

Cutlip, S., Center, A., & Broom, G. (1999). *Effective public relations*. Prentice Hall.

Edwards, L. (2018). *Understanding public relations: Theory, culture and society*. SAGE Publications.

Edwards, L., & Hodges, C. E. (2011). Introduction: Implications of a (radical) socio-cultural "turn" in public relations scholarship. In *Public relations, society & culture* (pp. 1–14). Routledge.

Elliott, I., Fejszes, V., & Tàrrega, M. (2019). The Community Empowerment Act and localism under devolution in Scotland: The perspective of multiple stakeholders in a council ward. *International Journal of Public Sector Management, 32*(3), 302–319.

Escobar, O. (2017). Pluralism and democratic participation: What kind of citizen are citizens invited to be? *Contemporary pragmatism, 14*(4), 416–438.

Fernández-Cavia, J. (2011). Ciudades, regiones y países como marcas. Luces y sombras del place branding. In J. San Eugenio Vela (coord.), *Manual de comunicación turística: de la información a la persuasión, de la promoción a la emoción* (pp. 103–113). Documenta Universitaria.

Fernández-Cavia, J., & Huertas, A. (2014). La gestión de las marcas de destino y de territorio desde la perspectiva de las relaciones públicas. *Comunicació: revista de recerca I d'anàlisi, 31*(1), 9–26.

Grunig, J. E. (1992) (ed.). *Excellence in Public Relations and Communication management*. Lawrence Erlbaum Associates.

Ginesta, X., San Eugenio, J., Corral, J. A., & Montaña, J. (2020). The role of a city council in a place branding campaign: The case of Vic in Catalonia. *Sustainability, 12*(11), 4420.

Govers, R., & Go, F. (2009). *Place branding: Glocal, virtual and physical identities, constructed, imagined and experienced*. Palgrave Macmillan.

Jiménez Morales, M., & San Eugenio, J. (2011). Identidad territorial y promoción turística: la organización de eventos como estrategia de creación, consolidación y difusión de la imagen de marca del territorio. *ZER: Revista De Estudios De Comunicación/ Komunikazio Ikasketen Aldizkaria, 14*(26), 277–297.

Kavaratzis, M., & Kalandides, A. (2015). Rethinking the place brand: The interactive formation of place brands and the role of participatory place branding. *Environment and Planning, 47*(6), 1368–1382.

Kemp, E., Williams, K., & Bordelon, B. (2012). The impact of marketing on internal stakeholders in destination branding: The case of a musical city. *Journal of Vacation Marketing, 18*(2), 121–133.

L'Etang, J., Hodges, E. M., & Pieczka, M. (2012). Cultures and places: Ethnography in public relations spaces. *Public Relations Review, 38*(4), 519–521.

L'Etang, J., & Pieczka, M. (2006). *Public relations: Critical debates and contemporary practice.* Routledge.

López-Lita, R., & Benlloch, M.T. (2005). De la marca comercial a la marca territorio. *Recerca: Revista de pensament i anàlisi, 5*, 87–100.

Lucarelli, A. (2018). Place branding as urban policy: The (im)political place branding. *Cities, 80*, 12–21.

Ma, W., Daan, S., Bruijne, M., Jong, M., & Lu, H. (2019). Tracing the Origins of Place Branding Research: A Bibliometric Study of Concepts in Use (1980–2018). *Sustainability, 11*(11), 2999. https://doi.org/10.3390/su11112999

Moilanen, T., & Rainisto, S. (2009). *How to brand nations, cities and destinations: A planning book for place branding.* Palgrave Macmillan.

Papadopoulos, N. (2004). Place branding: Evolution, meaning and implications. *Place Branding, 1*(1), 36–49.

Pieczka, M. (2015). Dialogue and critical public relations. In J. L'Etang, D. McKie, N. Snow, & J. Xifra (Eds.), *The Routledge handbook of critical public relations* (pp. 76–89). Routledge.

Piñeiro-Naval, V., & Igartua Perosanz, J. J. (2012). La difusión del patrimonio a través de Internet. El caso de Castilla y León. *Cuadernos de Turismo*, (30), 191-217.

Robson, P. (2021). Public relations and place branding: Friend, foe or just ignored? A systematic review. *Public Relations Review, 47*(5), Art. 102096.

San Eugenio, J. (2011). *La transformació de territoris en marques: el reconeixement i la diferenciació d'identitats espacials en temps postmoderns. Un estat de la qüestió* [Doctoral Thesis]. Universitat Pompeu Fabra.

San Eugenio, J., Ginesta, X., Compte-Pujol, M., & Frigola-Reig, J. (2019). Building a place brand on local assets: The case of the Pla de l'Estany district and its rebranding. *Sustainability, 11*(11), 3218.

San Eugenio, J., Ginesta, X., Compte-Pujol, M., Frigola-Reig, J., & Fernández-Rovira, C. (2023). Local and sustainable production as vectors of an agrarian branding strategy in Catalonia: Case study of the Baixa Tordera. *Journal of Place Management and Development, 16*(3), 329–346.

San Eugenio, J., Ginesta, X., & Kavaratzis, M. (2019). The critical role of stakeholder engagement in a place branding strategy: A case study of the Empordà brand. *European Planning Studies*, *28*(7), 1393–1412.

Sintomer, Y., Herzberg, C., & Röcke, A (2008). Participatory budgeting in Europe: Potentials and challenges. *International Journal of Urban and Regional Research*, *32*(1), 164–178.

Skinner, H. (2021). Place branding—The challenges of getting it right: Coping with success and rebuilding from crises. *Tourism and Hospitality*, *2*(1), 173–189.

Swain, S., Jebarajakirthy, C., Sharma, B. K., Maseeh, H. I., Agrawal, A., Shah, J., & Saha, R. (2023). Place branding: A systematic literature review and future research agenda. *Journal of Travel Research*, *63*(3), 535–564.

Theunissen, P., & Wan Norbani, W. N. (2012). Revisiting the concept "dialogue" in public relations. *Public Relations Review*, *38*(1), 5–13.

Van Assche, K., Beunen, R., & Oliveira, E. (2020). Spatial planning and place branding: Rethinking relations and synergies. *European Planning Studies*, *28*(7), 1274–1290.

Vuignier, R. (2017). Place branding & place marketing 1976–2016: A multidisciplinary literature review. *International Review on Public and Nonprofit Marketing*, *14*(4), 447–473.

Antonio Castillo-Esparcia, Elizabet Castillero-Ostio, and Andrea Moreno-Cabanillas

Lobbies and pressure groups: Analyzing revolving doors in Spain's public relations

Abstract: The field of public relations covers many activities within organizations, including relations with public authorities. In this aspect, communication strategies with public institutions are organized through lobbies or pressure groups.

One of the most characteristic actions of these political actors is that of the revolving doors as a mechanism for access to and knowledge of the workings of public authorities. In Spain, despite attempts to regulate these activities, a significant number of cases continue to occur. In this research, through a content analysis, we have analyzed the cases of revolving doors—in which people have migrated from the public to the private sphere—in Spain over the last 50 years, making it possible to show the strong link between the elites of political power and business power.

Keywords: Public relations, political communication, lobby, revolving door

1. Introduction

Public relations, in the context of political communication, is used to build and maintain a favorable image of the politician, party or institution, as well as to establish and strengthen the relationship with citizens and other key actors. This involves the development of clear and consistent messages, the selection of appropriate communication channels and the adoption of a strategic approach to information dissemination.

Taking into account the various political actors, among the organizational typologies that can be found, lobbies are entities specialized in the management of influence toward public authorities (Castillo, 2011). Although their influence may vary and their participation may pose challenges, interest groups or lobbies play a fundamental role in the representation of various sectors of society and in the course of political decision-making. In the communication process between these political actors and institutions, two types of communication actions are usually implemented: direct lobbying and grassroots lobbying. These actions aim to promote certain policies or causes and to persuade legislators or decision-makers in favor of their interests. Both strategies can be complementary and used together to maximize influence on public institutions. Direct lobbying seeks direct and personalized interaction with decision-makers through meetings or advice, while grassroots lobbying aims to create popular support and pressure from the grassroots, taking into account the mediating role of the media, citizen demonstrations or debates, among other actions (Kollman, 1998; Somerville, 2011; Xifra, 2009).

Some research has highlighted the significant role of relationships between political elites and lobbyists, as well as the impact that these links can have on lobbying strategies (Ørsten et al., 2017). One of the phenomena that has been studied in this context is that of "revolving doors."

2. Theoretical framework

"Revolving doors" refers to the practice whereby people who have held political or government positions move on to work as professional lobbyists or in private companies, and vice versa. This creates a direct connection between policymakers and lobbyists, which can influence public decisions. Bringing in a former government official can, in some cases, bring benefits in terms of influence and political knowledge. Hiring a former official who has worked in government can provide a direct connection to the political environment and internal networks (Baumgartner et al., 2009; Makse, 2017). These links can be valuable for understanding government processes, and studies show that revolving-door lobbying is more successful than non-revolving-door lobbying for several reasons: because it can access up-to-date information and possess expert knowledge about public policy procedure (Cerrillo-i-Martínez, 2017; LaPira & Thomas, 2017; Makse, 2017; Parker et al. 2012), knowing which legislative staff are most attuned to business projects, when is the right time to access them, as well as what to say and how in a future meeting (McKay & Lazarus, 2023), as well as having a wider and more varied network of contacts with different legislative offices (Blanes et al., 2012; McCrain, 2018); but the fruit of these connections is subordinate to the tenure of colleagues within government (Strickland, 2019).

Revolving doors can affect the political decision-making process in four ways, according to Castellani (2018). On the one hand, politicians with the prospect of future employment opportunities in the private sector, who may be influenced by lobbying interests during their term of office, which may affect their objectivity and ability to make decisions in the public interest. And vice versa, private sector leaders who move to the public sector.

On the other hand, lobbyists and lobbying firms can leverage the connections and experience of former government officials to gain privileged access to and influence political decision-making. This can undermine transparency and fairness in the policy-making process, as the interests of certain groups may receive preferential treatment to the detriment of others (Vaquero & Cadaval, 2022). And in the opposite direction, from the public sector they move to lobbying firms.

The relationship between political elites and lobbyists through revolving doors has been the subject of debate and concern in many Western countries. Some nations have implemented regulations and restrictions to address this problem, such as mandatory cooling-off periods before former officials can work as lobbyists or limitations on post-public service employment contracts with limited results (Brezis & Cariolle, 2017). These measures aim to safeguard the integrity of the political process and ensure that decisions are taken impartially and for the benefit of society as a whole. In Spain, over the years, different measures have been implemented to address this issue through different initiatives:

1. Law 53/1984, of December 26, 1984, on Incompatibilities of personnel in the service of the Public Administrations: There is legislation that establishes the incompatibilities and conflicts of interest to which public officials are subject. This law establishes public restrictions to prevent politicians and civil servants from using their positions for personal or private gain.
2. Law 5/2006, of April 10, on the regulation of conflicts of interest of members of the Government and Senior Officials of the General State Administration.
3. Law 19/2013, of December 9, on Transparency, Access to Public Information and Good Governance.
4. Law 3/2015, of March 30, regulating the exercise of senior positions in the General State Administration (AGE).
5. Draft Bill on Transparency and Integrity in the Activities of Interest Groups with the aim of making the public administration more transparent and fostering public confidence (November 8, 2022).
6. Code of Good Practices: There are codes of conduct and good practices that seek to regulate revolving doors and promote transparency in relations between the public and private sectors.
7. Conflict of Interest Commission: A commission has been created for this purpose, as an independent body in charge of monitoring and resolving potential conflict of interest situations in the political and administrative sphere. This committee evaluates specific cases and issues recommendations or opinions on the situations raised.

It is important to highlight that, despite these initiatives, the revolving-door phenomenon continues to be the subject of criticism and debate in Spain, given that the regulation in this regard is not fully defined, with various regulations and projects in force that aim to make the process transparent, but with a need for improvement in their implementation.

Bearing in mind that the regulation of revolving doors has had loopholes that it has not been able to cover over the last few decades, it is necessary to investigate the possible cases that have occurred.

3. Methodology

At the methodological level, this study adopted an analytical-descriptive approach, from a quantitative perspective, through content analysis, to analyze possible cases of revolving doors in the last 50 years in Spain. This contribution has focused on the types of outgoing revolving doors—where the person moves from working in the public to the private sector—as identified by Castellani (2018), as described by the OECD:

> public officials move to lucrative private sector positions that they come from regulating, where they can use their government experience and accumulated connections or networks, for personal and/or their new employer's benefit to the detriment of the public sector and/or other private sector competitors.

With the main objective in mind, the following secondary objectives (SO, hereafter) are pursued:

- SO1: To find out the percentage of women and men who have worked in the public sector and have moved to private sector positions, and to analyze the position they hold or have held.
- SO2: Determine the business sectors in which the practice of revolving doors is most prevalent.
- SO3: To examine which high-ranking national or regional officials, as well as officials considered influential in the political sphere, have moved to the private sector and what type of position they have subsequently held in this organization.
- SO4: To distinguish other types of revolving exit doors in the field of public administration other than politics.

In order to achieve the objectives, the data collection has been marked by two search systems:

1. The first 100 private companies in the ranking offered by the digital newspaper Crónica Global (n.d.), based on official data from the commercial registers, which shows the 15,000 leading companies in Spain, were traced. Initially, we turned to the corporate website of these companies, to the section that shed light on the composition of the board of directors, corporate governance or even the management committee. Based on this information, a study was

made of the curricula vitae of the personnel detected in order to determine whether there had previously been any political or other type of relationship with the public administration in any sphere. In addition to this current search, a search for these same companies was carried out in the Google news search engine, using the keywords "revolving doors" or "revolving door" + "the name of the company," in order to determine possible situations that may have occurred prior to the present day.

2. Using the digital tool "Mynews"—hemeroteca digital at prensa—a search was carried out with the same terms used previously "revolving doors" or "revolving door" in the Spanish press; this time without applying any company, in order to obtain the possibility of other cases different from those already detected in the previous system.

The sampling has been intentional, based on the ranking of the companies with the highest turnover, and therefore with the greatest possibilities for the placement of public officials, as well as a search based only on the terms considered to be the focus of this research.

In the absence of previous methodological models that were fully adapted to the objectives pursued in this study, an analysis template of our own was designed, in which variables and categories designed ad hoc were taken into account (Table 1).

Table 1. Analysis template

Gender	Business sector	Position held within the organization	Higher national and regional public officials/other influential political officials	Non-political position held within the public administration
Male	Energy	1st level board of administration: President/ Vice-president/General Secretary.	President	Tax Inspector
Female	Banking/Finance	2nd level board of directors: Councilor/ Vocal	Vice-President	State Lawyer

(*continued*)

Table 1. Continued

Gender	Business sector	Position held within the organization	Higher national and regional public officials/other influential political officials	Non-political position held within the public administration
	Telecommunications/ Technology	3rd level Board of Administration: External councilor/ Independent councilor/ Dominical councilor	Minister / Regional Councilor	State Ambassador
	Textile Retail	Management Committee: Executives	Member of Parliament / Senator	Head of Area or Technical Adviser
	Consulting	Adviser	Secretary of State	Other posts belonging to the general bodies/ scales of the Civil Service
	Automotive	Other	Undersecretary of State/Government Delegate	Other
	Food		Secretary Secretary/ General Technical/ Director General	
	Communication		Subdirector General	
	Construction		Mayor	
	Legal		Member of the Council of the CNMC/CNMV	
	Other		Political leader	
			Head of Cabinet and other advisers as temporary non-civil servant personnel	
			Other	

Source: authors' own.

In relation to the systematization of the data according to the analysis template, the following issues should be noted:

- If the person studied has held several different positions within the public sphere, in the processing of the data, the one that was from the political sphere was chosen before other positions belonging to the Civil Service. And within the political sphere, the most relevant one.
- If the person has covered several posts of the same category, the most current and closest to the date of occupation of the post in the private company was selected.
- High national/autonomous public posts and others of influence in the political sphere such as "chief of staff and other advisors as non-civil servant temporary staff" have been considered in the political post, given that they are occupations designated according to the person holding the political post and entail ideological proximity. The figure of "political leader or leader" has also been considered, who, although not belonging to the body of senior officials, does exert considerable influence from the political scene. CNMC and CNMV board members are also included in this category because they are considered senior officials.

The study sample is made up of 268 positions detected in 92 private organizations, resulting in 245 individuals identified as possible revolving-door cases. It is necessary to point out that for the treatment of the data, the research has been based on the posts or positions detected and not on the individuals, given that otherwise it is impossible to reach the data referring to the type of posts held in the organization or the diversity of sectors in which the companies studied are located, as the same person may have held posts of different categories in different companies.

4. Results

Taking into account the data referring to the sex of the people occupying the different positions of importance in the companies studied, it is worth noting that the male group is almost four times the female group (men, n=213; women= 55). Cross-referencing the data with the type of positions held by each of these individuals (see Figure 1), it is noteworthy that it is men who hold more positions classified as first-class, in terms of their degree of importance, on boards of directors. Only one woman—3.33 %—holds this rank, compared to 29 men—97.67 %.

On the other hand, Figure 1 shows how the male group occupies in the first place positions defined as second level—40.85 %—followed by those of third level—16.90 %—with first level positions within the board of directors and those representing managers remaining in third place, fairly evenly matched. On the other hand, the group made up of women holds the majority of third-level positions—36.36 %—followed by second-level positions—23.64 %—and third-level positions on the board of directors and other miscellaneous positions are tied with 18.18 %. Among these positions in the "other" category are: secretary to the board and not a board member, partner, collaborator or analyst.

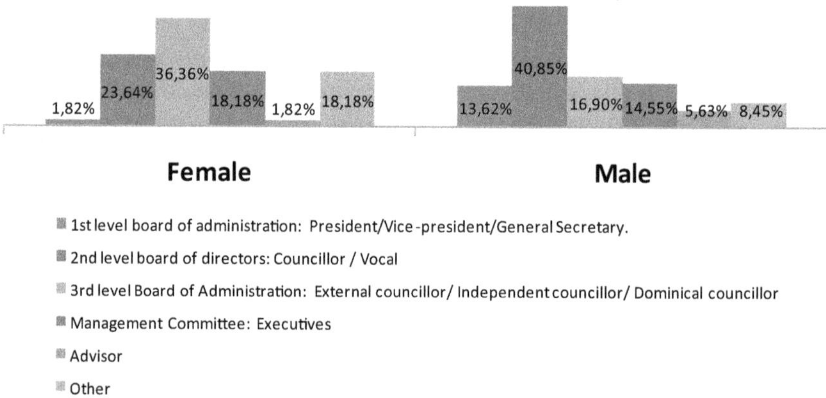

Figure 1. Gender distribution and position held within the organization.
Source: authors' own.

In the analysis of the sample of companies that have taken on staff who have been part of the public administration, the energy sector clearly prevails, given that it accounts for half of the companies that have recruited these people (see Figure 2). Of these, the following companies stand out as having offered the most posts to staff related to the public sector: Repsol (n=30), Enagás (n=23), Unión-Gas Natural Fenosa—predecessor of Naturgy—(n=19), Iberdrola (n= 16), Red Eléctrica de España (n=14) and Endesa (n=12). The communication sector and the banking/finance sector follow closely behind, tied at—7.84 %. The 9.33 % represents other sectors that have been in the minority and have been grouped in this category. These include sectors such as logistics and distribution, aeronautics, pharmaceuticals, armaments, real estate and hotels.

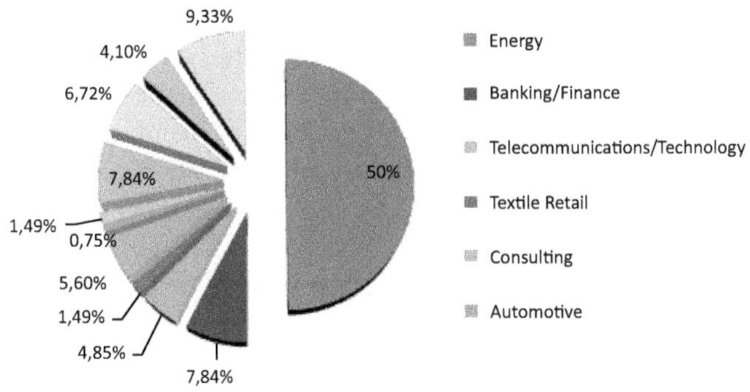

Figure 2. Distribution of the business sector to which the company belongs.
Source: authors' own.

Within this political sphere, ministers or, in the case of the regional sphere, regional councilors are the most prevalent persons in the positions of these companies (n=74; 31.49 %) (see Figure 3) followed by secretaries, technical secretaries general and directors general (n=54; 22.98 %) and in third place are the secretaries of state (n=23; 9.78 %). Also noteworthy are government vice presidents (n=13; 5.53 %) and presidents (n=10; 4.26 %), who occupy positions 6 and 7—intermediate positions in the categorized list.

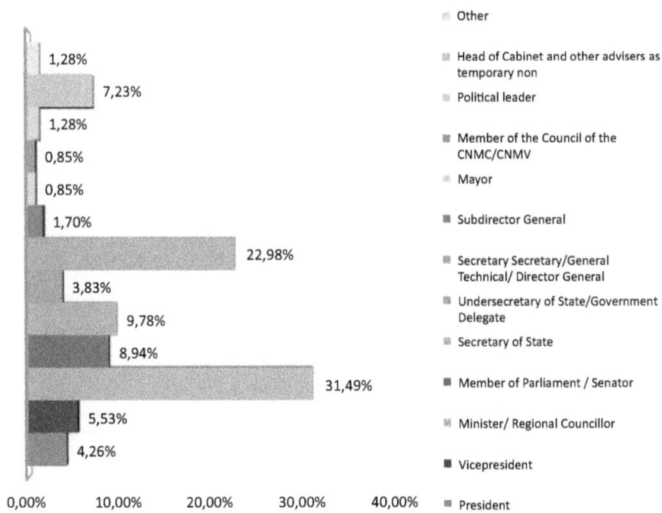

Figure 3. Distribution of national and regional senior public officials or other influential positions in the political sphere from which the people in the sample studied come.
Source: authors' own.

Contrasting the data on the political position held previously with the positions held subsequently in the business sphere (see Figure 4), it can be seen that the first and second-ranking positions are held by people who have held any of the political categories, except mayors or members of the Board of the CNMC or the CNMV, and the third-ranking positions, apart from those mentioned above, have not been held by vice-presidents, deputies, senators or general undersecretaries.

Distinguishing by category within the hierarchy of senior officials, it can be seen that ministers or councilors are the persons who hold the most first and second-ranking positions on the board of directors.

In addition, the analysis has uncovered 14 cases of possible revolving doors with international ramifications, such as the following situations: Benita Maria Ferrero-Waldner, a director of Unión-Gas Natural Fenosa, who has been Austrian Foreign Minister and European Commissioner for Trade and External Relations. Denise Patricia Kingsmill, a member of the current board of Inditex, who is a former member of the House of Lords in the United Kingdom. Henri Philippe Reichstul, current external director of Repsol, former Deputy Minister of Planning of Brazil. J. Robinson West, the current independent director of Repsol, who previously served as Under Secretary of the Interior and Under Secretary of Defence for International Economic Affairs in the United States. Luiz Fernando Furlan, who was a director of Telefónica and had previously been Minister of Industry in Brazil.

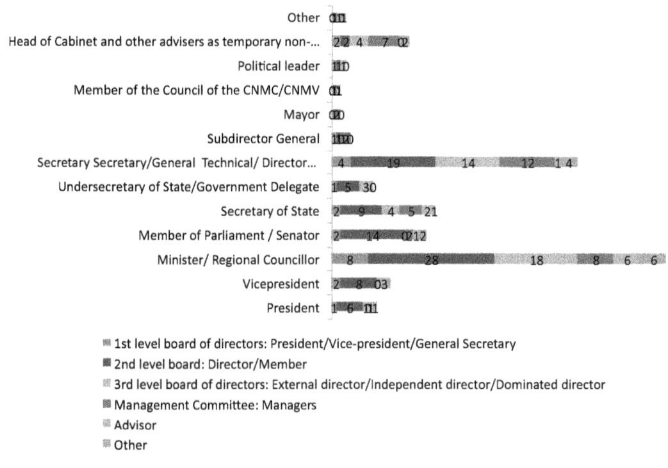

Figure 4. Comparison of previous public positions held and subsequent positions held in private enterprise.

Source: authors' own.

This study has also taken into account the sample made up of people who have held a post in the public administration, other than in the political sphere, and have subsequently migrated to the private sector (see Figure 5). It has been detected that the largest number is represented by state lawyers (30.30 %), with the category "others," represented by 42.42 % of the sample, combining posts such as directors or presidents of public companies or people belonging to the military scale.

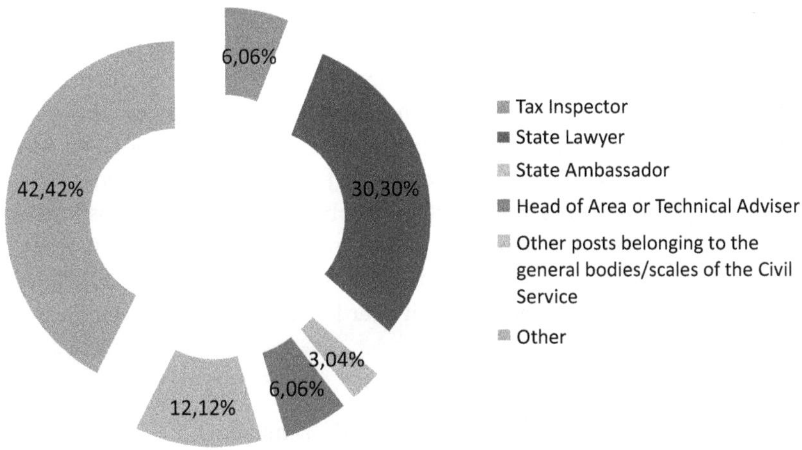

Figure 5. Study sample of persons who have held public office other than in the political sphere.
Source: authors' own.

5. Discussion and conclusion

Following the results obtained, and coinciding with previous research (Martínez-García et al., 2020; Palá, 2021; Santos & Palacios, 2021), this study confirms that it is the male group that holds the highest percentage of positions in private companies. Likewise, it is men who are better positioned in positions of greater relevance in these organizations compared to women, continuing the gender gap that has been occurring in recent years.

Clearly, the sector in which revolving doors are most prevalent is the energy sector, standing out from the rest of the sectors, given that it is the one that takes on the most public sector staff.

The study sample indicates that in the political category, which includes high-ranking national and regional public officials or other influential positions from the political sphere that have been transferred to the business sphere, there is a clear dominance of people who have previously been top-level authorities, such as ministers at national level or regional councilors at regional level, as well as holding the most important positions in the companies (first and second level within the board of directors). This fact clearly reveals how the best-placed political posts or the top positions in the institutional hierarchy result in better or more privileged occupations when they leave the business network.

This research has also revealed shifts from the public to the private sphere, not only at the national level but also at the international level with the occupation of positions in Spanish companies by people previously linked to the public-institutional environment in other countries.

Focusing attention on people who have been linked to the public administration outside the political sphere, the number of occasions on which they have obtained significant positions in the private sector is limited.

This study demonstrates the important links between the political-institutional power elites and business-economic power in Spain over the last 50 years. It highlights the different ministerial portfolios as possible fishing grounds from which private companies tend to recruit board members or managers.

References

Baumgartner, F. R., Berry, J. M., Hojnacki, M., Kimball, D. C., & Leech, B. L. (2009). *Lobbying and policy change: Who wins, who loses, and why*. University of Chicago Press.

Blanes i Vidal, J., Draca, M., & Fons-Rosen, C. (2012). Revolving door lobbyists. *The American Economic Review*, *102*(7), 3731–3748. https://doi.org/10.1257/aer.102.7.3731

Brezis, E. S., & Cariolle, J. (2017). Financial sector regulation and the revolving door in US commercial banks. In N. Schofield & G. Caballero (Eds.), *State, institutions and democracy. Contributions of political economy* (pp. 53–76). Springer.

Castellani, A. (2018). Lobbies y puertas giratorias. Los riesgos de la captura de la decisión pública. *Revista Nueva Sociedad*, *27*, 48–61. https://nuso.org/articulo/lobbies-y-puertas-giratorias/

Castillo, A. (2011). *Lobby y comunicación: el lobbying como estrategia comunicativa*. Comunicación Social.

Cerrillo-i-Martínez, A. (2017). Beyond revolving doors: The prevention of conflicts of interests through regulation. *Public Integrity*, *19*(4), 357–373. https://doi.org/10.1080/10999922.2016.1225479

Kollman, K. (1998). *Outside lobbying: Public opinion and interest group strategies.* Princeton University Press.

LaPira, T. M., & Thomas, H. F. (2017). *Revolving door lobbying: Public service, private influence, and the unequal representation of interests.* University Press of Kansas.

Makse, T. (2017). A very particular set of skills: Former legislator traits and revolving-door lobbying in congress. *American Politics Research*, *45*(5), 866–886. https://doi.org/10.1177/1532673X16677274

Martínez-García, I., Sacristán-Navarro, M., & Gómez-Ansón, S. (2020). Diversidad de género en los consejos de administración: El efecto de la normativa en la presencia de mujeres en las empresas españolas cotizadas. *Revista Internacional de Investigación en Comunicación aDResearch ESIC*, *22*(22), 60–81. https://revistasinvestigacion.esic.edu/adresearch/index.php/adresearch/article/view/150/326

McCrain, J. (2018). Revolving door lobbyists and the value of congressional staff connections. *Journal of Politics*, *80*(4), 1369–1383. https://doi.org/10.1086/698931

McKay, A. M., & Lazarus, J. (2023). Policy consequences of revolving-door lobbying. *Political Research Quarterly*, *76*(4), 1780–1793. https://doi.org/10.1177/10659129231177648

Ørsten, M. B., Willig, I., & Pederson, L. H. (2017). PR, lobbyism and democracy: Mapping the revolving door in Denmark from 1981 to 2015. *Nordicom Review*, *38*(2), 19–31. https://doi.org/10.1515/nor-2017-0405

Palá Laguna, R. (2021). La diversidad de género en el consejo de administración y en la alta dirección de las sociedades cotizadas. *Revista Aragonesa de Administración Pública*, *56*, 41–62. https://dialnet.unirioja.es/servlet/articulo?codigo=7971152

Parker, G. R., Parker, S. L., & Dabros, M. S. (2012). The labor market for politicians: Why ex-legislators gravitate to lobbying. *Business & Society*, *52*(3), 427–450. http://dx.doi.org/10.1177/0007650312465579

Santos Jaén, J. M., & Palacios Muñoz, A. (2021). Igualdad de género en los consejos de administración ¿Realidad o utopía? *La Razón Histórica. Revista hispanoamericana de Historia de las Ideas*, *51*, 16–40. https://www.revistalarazonhistorica.com/51-2/

Somerville, I. (2011). Managing public affairs and lobbying: Persuasive communication in the policy sphere. In D. Moss & B. DeSanto (Eds.), *Public relations: A managerial perspective* (pp. 167–192). SAGE Publications.

Strickland, J. M. (2019). The declining value of revolving-door lobbyists: Evidence from the American states. *American Journal of Political Science*, *64*(1), 67–81. https://doi.org/10.1111/ajps.12485

Vaquero García, A., & Cadaval Sampedro, M. (2022). Reflexiones y propuestas para combatir la corrupción pública en la administración local. *Revista Española de Transparencia*, *15*, 181–205. https://doi.org/10.51915/ret.219

Xifra, J. (2009). *Els lobbies*. Editorial UOC.

Part Three Local Contexts and Global Trends in Public Relations

Ana Belén Fernández-Souto, Montse Vázquez Gestal, and Iván Puentes-Rivera

Analysis of the communication structures of Spanish clusters in Spain (2017–2022)

Abstract: The main objective of this chapter is to understand the communicative evolution of business conglomerates in Spain and analyze the impact that COVID-19 has had on their structure and operation. Studying how professionals in the sector have adapted their working situation in the last five years provides an overall picture that serves as a starting point for understanding the current state of organizational communication in our country and provides conclusions that are not far from those of other studies in the professional field of communication: professionalization in this field is still a challenge, both in terms of the structure of internal communication departments and in terms of the level of education of their managers; and the outsourcing of services continues to be crucial, particularly in digital services and event organization.

Keywords: cluster, company, communication, department, office, Spain

1. Introduction

The reality of business communication in Spain has been periodically analyzed from different fields, which makes it possible to evaluate the progress and challenges facing the profession.

From an academic point of view, this study aims to help to understand the evolution of this activity and does so through the analysis of the communicative structure of existing business clusters in Spain. Starting from a study published in 2018, five years later, this article will show the results of the historical analysis and will provide continuity to broader research that maps organizational communication in different business and institutional sectors in our country.

2. Theoretical framework

2.1 Clusters as business conglomerates

According to the European Union, a business cluster is a group of independent companies, as well as research and knowledge dissemination organizations and other related economic actors, designed to stimulate activity by promoting the exchange of facilities, knowledge, and experience. Close to this concept is the

AEI (which stands for Innovative Business Group in Spanish), which results from the combination, in a geographical area or productive sector, of companies and public or private research and training centers involved in a collaborative exchange process aimed at obtaining advantages and/or benefits derived from the execution of joint projects of an innovative nature (https://clusters.ipyme.org/es-es/PoliticaClusters/Informacion/Paginas/QueEsCluster.aspx).

In both cases, their creation brings benefits for the companies that constitute them and for the region that hosts them, since they increase productivity by taking advantage of synergies, foster innovation and stimulate the creation of new companies.

These organizations, as conglomerates of companies, work as lobby entities to optimize and capture resources (economic and human); for this, the strategic management of their communication is essential and must be planned and organized according to the founding objectives of the cluster.

This will be the objective of this chapter, which aims to collect data on the reality of the communication of existing clusters in Spain in 2022 and 2017.

2.2 Academic background

In this framework, this research studies the prevailing communication structure in the different Spanish clusters.

In Spain there has been academic research on the organizational reality of some clusters (Giménez Rivera, 2019; Sánchez García, 2021; Martínez-Murcia, 2019), but it focuses on very specific sectors or studies economic and financial aspects (Peco-Lahuerta et al., 2019; De-Lourdes-Cárcamo-Solís et al., 2019; De-La-Torre-Palacios, 2022). There are also studies at the European level, especially those carried out by the Cluster Observatory (https://clustercollaboration.eu/tags/european-cluster-observatory). However, they are focused on economic and financial analysis and the last edition was published in 2015.

On the other hand, there are several studies on communication management and the professional profile of managers in specific areas, such as large companies (Fernández-Souto et al., 2019a; Moreno & Capriotti, 2006), small and medium-sized businesses (Fernández-Souto, 2005; Fernández-Souto & Puentes-Rivera, 2014), polluting companies (Fernández-Souto et al., 2015, 2019b, universities and research centers (Simón Onieva, 2015), city councils (Fernández-Souto & Vázquez Gestal, 2014) or NGOs (Salvador i Peris, 1999), among others. We also highlight the existence of larger studies, such as the one carried out by Dircom, which compiles data on all types of organizations. As for business clusters, there is only one scientific publication from 2018 (Fernández-Souto, Puentes-Rivera and Vázquez Gestal) focusing on communication within these structures, and this article aims to provide current data that allow a comparative study and to know how it has evolved in the past five years.

Of the existing reports and studies on the organization of communication structures in Spain, we highlight two that provide data on the overall picture of public and private organizations in our country: the Dircom and Euprera reports. Beyond the general overview of communication structures they provide, we believe that this article should also offer a reflection that goes beyond the structure of communication departments, and that raises the challenges that these structures face today.

2.3 Challenges facing the organizations' communicative structures

In this sense, one of the great challenges is the implementation of new technologies not only in the organization itself but also in the organizational structure of communication (Almansa-Martínez & Fernández-Souto, 2020). The pandemic has highlighted the value of the digital context, as even reluctant organizations were compelled to opt for online formats to serve their audiences. The spreading of these technologies has fostered scenarios in which digital modes of connection and communication permeate all aspects of our lives. Public relations and communication have not been unaffected by these changes. The specialized literature reveals that Spanish organizations are gradually discovering the advantages of the digital arena to manage it (Cuenca-Fontbona et al., 2020). In this context, the communication strategies and structures have been forced to evolve and the comparison between these clusters' departments in the last five years will provide evidence of this. The arrival of these technologies forces professionals to incorporate new competencies into their jobs (Rodríguez-Fernández & Vázquez-Sande, 2019).

It is also necessary to rethink the role that managers give communication in their internal organization chart. Internal communication professionals and academics increasingly conceive it as a key strategic value for organizations (ACEDEC, 2019). In this context, the role of the communications director is essential, as pointed out by Miquel-Segarra and Aced-Toledano (2019), so their specific training in this area is crucial. The communications director must lead the change and set out the organization's strategy, based on transparency and accountability. To achieve this, it is essential that they are committed to professionalization and stand against the unqualified practice of the profession. This trend is already evident in the *Informe PR 2018* (PRnoticias, 2018), a report that shows that in Spain the number of professional affiliations is increasing. As pointed out by Almansa-Martínez (2015), "training becomes the backbone of any professional working in communication." The Public Relations professional has to be trained to interact with the media, but also to be at the forefront of internal communication, crisis communication, protocol or interact with specialized audiences, lobbies, among other areas of activity (Castillo-Esparcia, Guerra-Heredia, et al., 2017; Castillo-Esparcia, Smolak et al., 2017). Of course, leadership skills to integrate the whole team in the medium-to-long-term strategic vision of the organization are essential for the success of the department as such.

Without these qualities, the communicative success of the organization would be left to chance and, therefore, its own success or even its survival could be called into question.

3. Methodology and objectives

As stated above, this chapter responds to a comparative study between the data collected five years ago and the present, and beyond this comparison, both shared some objectives:

MO (Main Objective): The fundamental objective of this research is to draw a general overview of communication management as carried out by Spanish clusters or business conglomerates in 2017 and 2022, analyzing the resources available to them, the most common practices, and the degree of professionalization of this work within them.

The specific objectives include:

O.1. To find out how the communication departments of these conglomerates are organized.
O.2. To carry out a comparative study on the organization of these departments between 2017 and 2022.
O.3. To analyze the academic background of communication managers.
O.4. To compare the evolution of the academic training of these managers over the past five years.
O.5. To analyze the degree of outsourcing of communication services.
O.6. To comparatively study this degree of outsourcing of communication services.

To meet the stated objectives, we must point out that two similar methodologies have been followed in both phases of the research:

- 2018 study: In the absence of an official registry of clusters, a webographic mapping of the clusters according to the geographical distribution by autonomous communities was carried out. To narrow it down, the public listings provided by some regions were analyzed, as is the case of Andalusia, Asturias, Catalonia, Extremadura, Galicia, La Rioja, Madrid, Murcia, and the Basque Country. In those instances where the autonomous governments lacked a specific registry, an Internet search was carried out using the parameters "autonomous community + cluster." Ultimately, the object of study was limited to 178 clusters, of which 129 were contacted, representing 60 % of the total.

- 2023 study: The study universe was defined as all the existing clusters in Spain. To contact all of them, the database provided by the Spanish Ministry of Industry, Trade and Tourism on the Innovative Business Clusters website (https://clusters.ipyme.org/es-es/Paginas/PagInicio.aspx) was used and a search was carried out for all registered entities, covering all sectors and autonomous communities, up to a total of 106 as shown in Table 1. Of these, 89 responses were obtained, representing 86 % of the total.

Table 1. Clusters included in the AEI Cluster of the Spanish Ministry of Industry, Trade and Tourism

Autonomous community	**Number of clusters registered with AEI**
Andalusia	6
Aragon	13
Asturias	6
The Balearic Islands	1
The Canary Islands	2
Cantabria	1
Castille and Leon	6
Catalonia	24
Valencian Community	9
Galicia	8
Madrid	10
Murcia	1
Navarra	6
The Basque Country	9
La Rioja	4
Total	106

Made by the authors from https://clusters.ipyme.org/es-es/Identificar/Paginas/ListadoAEI.aspx

In both 2018 and 2023, once the list had been compiled, the clusters under study were contacted to conduct a telephone interview with the communication managers or, alternatively, the managers of the organization, who were asked about their organizational chart and the organization of the cluster's communication, the training of the communication managers in the cluster, the existence of a specific communication plan and, finally, the outsourcing of communication services. These interviews were carried out in the periods of September–October 2022 and January–March 2017. From there, an analysis of the data obtained was carried out and charts were made to facilitate the understanding of the results and conclusions.

4. Results

The reality of clusters in Spain has changed greatly in the last five years. While a total of 178 clusters were identified in the study published in 2018, they were not officially registered. Five years later, there is an inventory by the Spanish government that lists up to 106.

Considering this data, it is obvious that some of the clusters analyzed in the first batch no longer appear in the second batch, either due to their disappearance, the creation of new clusters or an excessively broad consideration of the concept of cluster in the 2018 study, since in the absence of an official list that brings together these clusters of companies, no specific criteria were required of them beyond the use of the term "cluster" in their name.

Despite this limitation, the research has obtained the following results:

Comparing the data collected in the research, it is evident that the number of clusters that have an internal communication department has increased by 15 points. This reality suggests that organizations understand the need to invest in communication and are committed to the creation of specific structures to take on these tasks. In this regard, it should be noted that these communication departments should take on management and leadership tasks for the organization, so their position within the organizational chart should be close to the head of the organization (Figure 1).

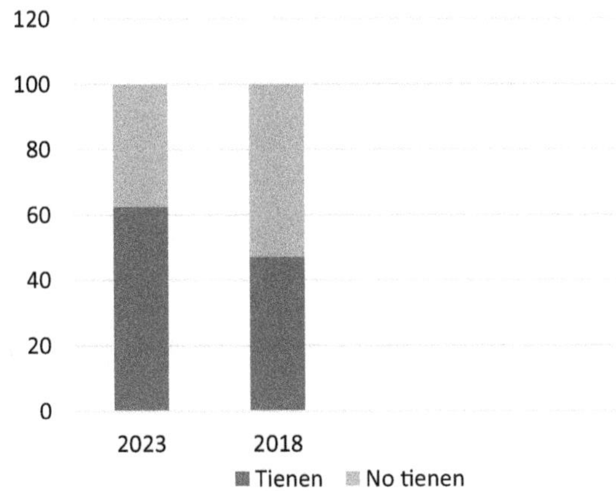

Figure 1. Comparison of the existence of specific communication departments in the clusters analyzed.

Source: authors' own.

In this sense, the latest edition of the Dircom study reflects the reality at a global level in Spanish companies and institutions. We understand that most of the clusters analyzed would fall into the category of less than 25 employees or, at most, 25–100 employees, so the data extracted from our research is in line with that presented by Dircom (Figure 2 and Figure 3).

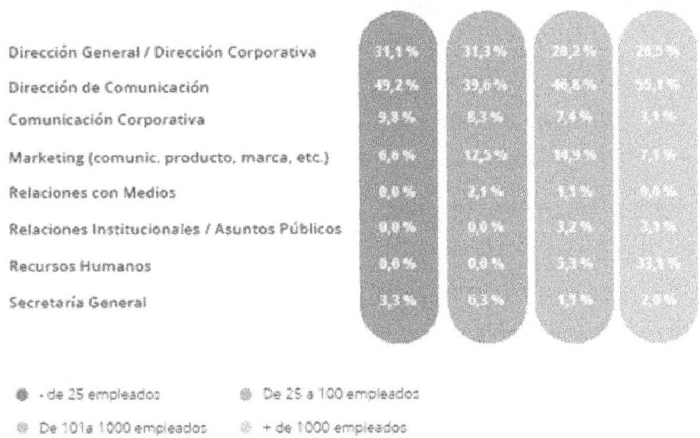

Figure 2. Position of the communication role within the company structure according to the number of company employees.

Source: DIRCOM. Estado de la comunicación en España 21–22.

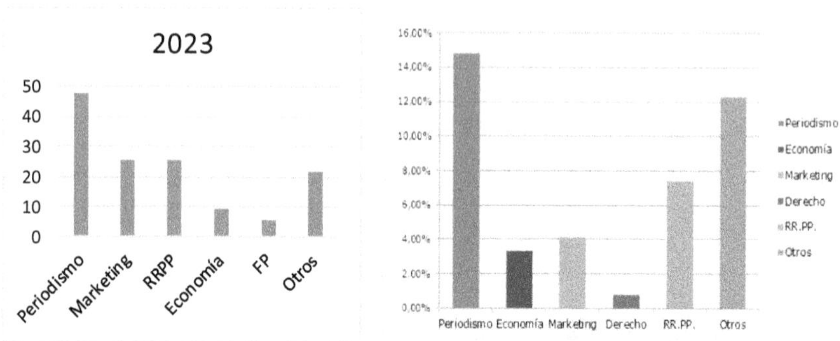

Figure 3. Comparison of the existence of specific communication departments in the analyzed clusters 2018–2023.

Source: authors' own.

In this comparison we see that the prevalence of journalists as leaders of the communication departments in the clusters studied is a constant in both 2018 and 2023, although it is true that they were not as present in the first part of the study, accounting for 14.7 % of the total while in 2023 it rises to 47.3 % (Figure 4).

Following Journalism, we also note that in both cases there is a high percentage of personnel trained in Publicity and Public Relations (12 % in 2018 and 25.5 % in 2023). In this case, an increase is identified in the latest phase of the study, in line with the data obtained from other studies, such as Dircom 21–22 (DIRCOM, Asociación de Directivos de Comunicación, 2022).

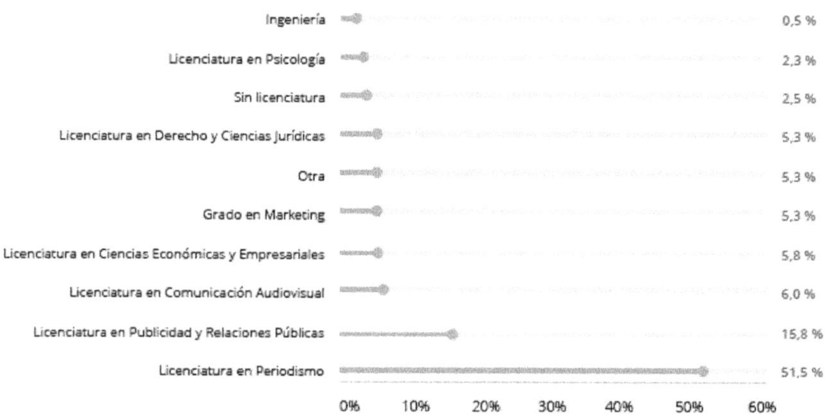

Figure 4. Fields of study of professionals according to their undergraduate training.

Source: Dircom, El estado de la comunicación en España 21–22.

Also worth mentioning is the presence of Marketing graduates, both in our study and in Dircom's, with a slight increase in the data collected in 2023 compared to that of 2018.

Regarding the remaining degrees of managers of communication departments, we highlight that Law has disappeared in 2023 and the percentage of other degrees has increased, which with 1.8 % of the total, includes degrees in Humanities, Statistics, Physics, Political Science, Architecture, Engineering, History, or International Business. Finally, in the data collected in 2023 it is worth highlighting the presence of people trained in Audiovisual Communication (up to 5.5 % of the total) and the emergence of personnel specialized in vocational training cycles, with the same percentage.

This data complements that presented in the Report on the State of Communication in Spain 21–22 on the academic qualifications of communication managers in the departments (Figure 5).

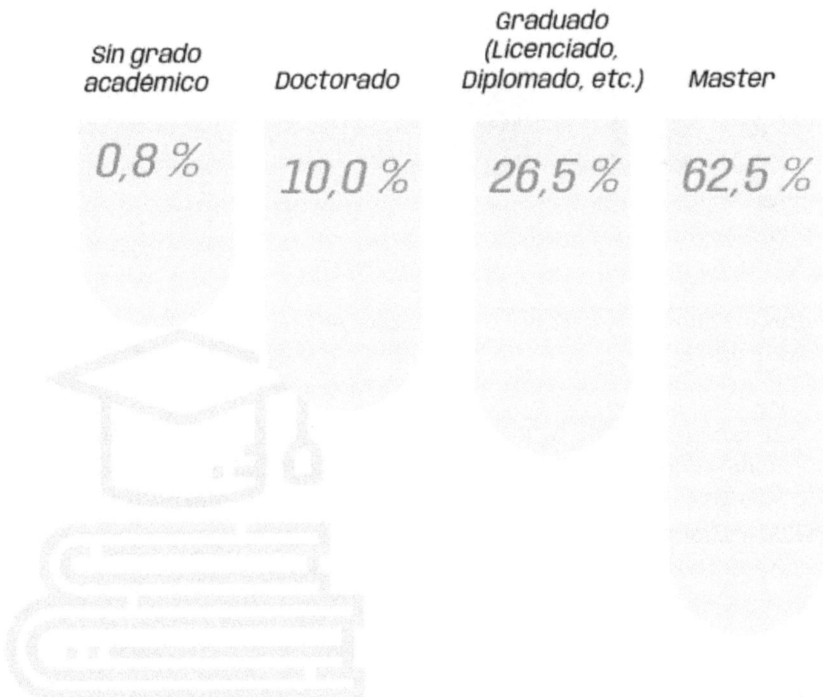

Figure 5. Academic background of the professionals.
Source: Dircom, El estado de la comunicación en España 21–22.

In the interviews, department heads were asked whether they outsourced communication services. The 2023 data clearly confirms this fact, which implies a professionalization of communication services, since they represent an increase of 20 points from the data collected in 2018. The structural reality of these departments is that, when they exist, they are understaffed, and, on many occasions, they do not have personnel with sufficient training to be able to plan and execute all the communicative actions and techniques. In this sense, it is confirmed that the current departments are aware of their limitations and turn to specialized external professionals to be able to undertake certain actions (Figure 6).

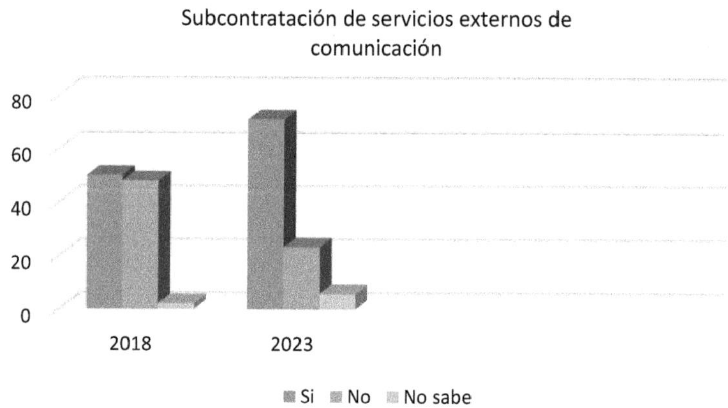

Figure 6. Outsourcing of external communication services.
Source: authors' own.

Considering this data, in 2023, clusters' communication managers were asked about the services they outsource, highlighting design and creative services (58.8 %), web and social media design and maintenance (cumulative 85.3 %) and media relations (39.7 %) (Figure 7).

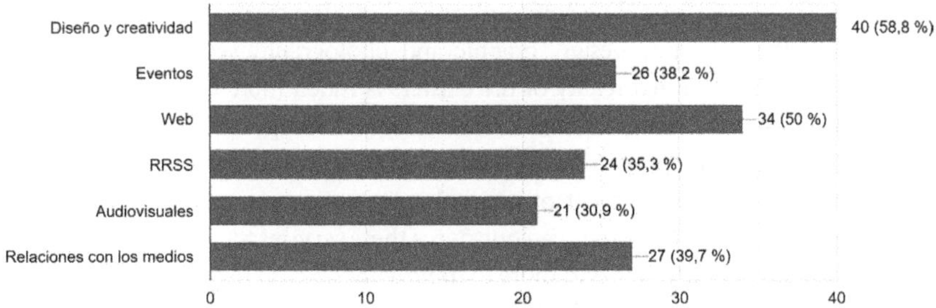

Figure 7. External communication services are outsourced by the clusters.
Source: authors' own.

This prioritization of actions matches those noted by the Dircom 21–22 study, which identifies the following as the most important communication areas for organizations (Figure 8).

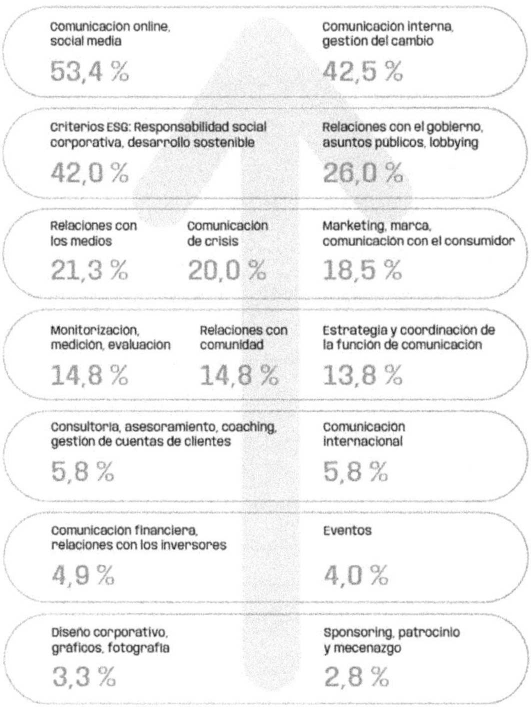

Figure 8. Trends in the areas of communication.
Source: Dircom, El estado de la comunicación en España 21–22.

Therefore, we see that online communication leads the overall market trend with 53.4 %, but the corporate design, graphic and photography section only has 3.3 %. Given that the analyzed reality of the clusters is much more limited in terms of economic and human resources, we understand that the importance they give to the outsourcing of design services is paramount for them, since most of their departments are focused on the management of internal communication, media relations and event organization, although they can outsource these services too. The reality of their day-to-day work tends to respond more to improvisation than to strategic planning.

Finally, the latest edition of the Dircom report compares communication tasks today and in the next three years. In line with what was stated earlier, this reality cannot be extrapolated to the clusters analyzed, but it highlights some trends that may affect them and that we will aim to study in the future. Thus, an increase is identified in terms of internal communication, marketing and branding, public affairs, crisis communication, community relations, monitoring, but above all, corporate social responsibility and sustainable development (Figure 9).

	ACT	2024
Comunicación online, social media	57,5 %	53,4 %
Relaciones con los medios	55,3 %	21,3 %
Comunicación interna, gestión del cambio	30,8 %	42,5 %
Estrategia y coordinación de la función de comunicación	27,0 %	13,8 %
Marketing, marca, comunicación con el consumidor	19,5 %	18,5 %
Relaciones con el gobierno, asuntos públicos, lobbying	17,8 %	26,0 %
Comunicación de crisis	15,0 %	20,0 %
Responsabilidad social corporativa, desarrollo sostenible	14,8 %	42,0 %
Eventos	14,2 %	4,0 %
Diseño corporativo, gráficos, fotografía	9,0 %	3,3 %
Relaciones con la comunidad	8,0 %	14,8 %
Consultoría, asesoramiento, coaching, gestión de cuentas de clientes clave (internamente/externamente)	7,8 %	5,8 %
Monitorización, medición, evaluación	6,8 %	14,8 %
Comunicación internacional	6,5 %	5,8 %
Sponsoring, patrocinio y mecenazgo	1,8 %	2,8 %
Comunicación financiera, relaciones con los inversores	0,8 %	4,9 %

Figure 9. Comparison of tasks today and in the next three years.
Source: DIRCOM, El estado de la comunicación en España 21–22.

These trends are also reflected in the European Communication Monitor (2022), which highlights the need to build trust, invest in communication strategy and give continuity to social responsibility, among others (Figure 10).

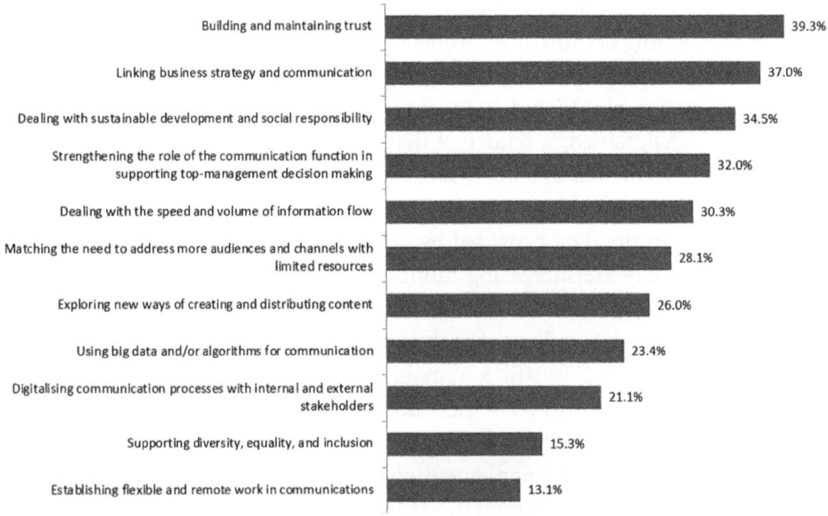

Figure 10. Strategic highlights of communication management until 2025.
Source: European Communication Monitor, 2022.

This highlights the day-to-day casuistry of the communications departments analyzed and the challenge of confirming whether their reality is catching up with that of other organizations in Spain.

5. Discussion and conclusions

As initially set out, this study has fulfilled its objectives in the sense that it has analyzed the reality of how communication is managed within clusters in Spain from a comparative analysis of the last five years (MO) considering the resources available to them, the most common practices, and the degree of professionalization in these organizations.

According to the data collected, the existence and consolidation of communication departments in Spanish clusters has improved compared to 2017 (O.1 and O.2). Even though this is a positive reference, we must be cautious about it since the object of study has evolved in the last five years and the sample is not a perfect match. In any case, this point is objective in terms of the reality in both years, and the improvement in the second phase of the study can be explained as the general trend of organizations to opt for strategic communication planning, as reported in other studies.

To complement this circumstance, the research set out the objective of analyzing the specific training of those responsible for the communication departments in the clusters (O.3. and O.4). A greater professionalization is not observed in the comparison between 2017 and 2022, but the trend of departments being led by journalists is maintained, a tendency that is also evident in other studies at a national level. On the other hand, there is still a high presence of communication directors who have not received specific training in this area, an issue that comes into conflict with the data provided by other reports, such as Dircom's, which highlight that there are increasing numbers of communication directors with higher education qualifications and the vast majority have a master's degree.

In any case, this data reflects that the professionalization of the departments of the clusters studied is still a remaining challenge, since many of these organizations do not consider it necessary to create an internal structure to manage their communication and image.

On the other hand, and complementing the previous data, the outsourcing of communication services continues to be fundamental to manage communication within the cluster and there have been considerable developments over the past five years (O.5 and O.6). This aspect is relevant in the sense that these organizations detect that it is necessary to carry out communicative actions but do not have sufficient internal resources to do so without outsourcing. In this sense, the techniques and tools they outsource the most are those related to design and creativity, online services (mainly web services) and relations with the media, which coincides with the trend of other organizations, according to reports such as Dircom's.

References

ADECEC. (2019). *La comunicación interna. Gran aliada en los nuevos modelos de negocio*. Asociación de Empresas Consultoras en Relaciones Públicas y Comunicación. http://adecec.com/wp-content/uploads/2019/03/CI_ADECEC.pdf

Almansa-Martínez, A. (2015). *Formación de profesionales estratégicos* (p. 84). Anuario de la comunicación. Dircom. https://www.dircom.org/boletin/anuario2015/boletin-anuario-2015.html?acm=1834_243

Almansa-Martínez, A., & Fernández-Souto, A. B. (2020). Professional Public Relations (PR) trends and challenges. *El profesional de la información*, 29(3). https://doi.org/10.3145/epi.2020.may.03

Castillo-Esparcia, A., Guerra-Heredia, S., & Almansa-Martínez, A. (2017). Comunicación política y think tanks en España. Estrategias con los medios de comunicación. *El profesional de la información, 26*(4). https://doi.org/10.3145/epi.2017.jul.14

Cuenca-Fontbona, J., Matilla, K., & Compte-Pujol, M. (2020). Transformación digital de los departamentos de relaciones públicas y comunicación de una muestra de empresas españolas. *Revista de Comunicación, 19*(1). https://doi.org/10.26441/RC19.1-2020-A5

De-La-Torre-Palacios, L. (2022). El sector minero español buscando su futuro: estrategias de abastecimiento y de clúster de desarrollo. *Cuadernos de estrategia, 209*, 281–324.

De-Lourdes-Cárcamo-Solís, M., Serrano-Torres, M. G., & Márquez-de-Anda, C. (2019). Fortalecimiento del cluster de calzado como estrategia para el desarrollo regional. Análisis México-España. In *DESARROLLO Y RESPONSABILIDAD SOCIAL* (p. 83). Academia de Ciencias Administrativas.

DIRCOM, Asociación de Directivos de Comunicación. (2015). *Estado de la Comunicación en España 2015*. DIRCOM. https://www.youtube.com/watch?v=At7Fakd1H3k

DIRCOM, Asociación de Directivos de Comunicación. (2022). *Estado de la Comunicación en España 2021-22*. Dircom.

EUROPEAN COMMUNICATION MONITOR. (2022). *Exploring diversity and empathy in leadership, Comtech and consulting in communications. Results of a survey in 43 countries*. https://www.communicationmonitor.eu/2022/07/07/ecm-european-communication-monitor-2022/

Fernández-Souto, A. B. (2005). Situación de los gabinetes de comunicación en organizaciones privadas en la provincia de Pontevedra. Las zonas industriales versus zonas administrativas y comerciales. In P. Capriotti, A. Castillo, M. T. García, & J. Xifra (Eds.), *Tendencias Actuales en las Relaciones Públicas*. AIRP. http://airrpp.org/wp-content/uploads/2012/12/Actas-II-Congreso-AIRP.pdf

Fernández-Souto, A. B., Puentes-Rivera, I., & Vázquez-Gestal, M. (2019a). La gestión comunicativa de las grandes empresas en España: estructura, recursos y principales retos de sus responsables. *Communication & Society, 32*(1), 161–177.

Fernández-Souto, A. B., Puentes-Rivera, I., & Vázquez-Gestal, M. (2019b). Comunicación de los conglomerados de empresas en España. *Prisma social, 22*, 91–112.

Fernández-Souto, A. B., & Puentes-Rivera, I. (2014). Relaciones Públicas en la Pequeña y Mediana Empresa de Galicia: El Caso de la Zona Franca de Vigo. In K. Matilla (Ed.), *Cambio Social y Relaciones Públicas* (pp. 105–126). Edit UOC.

Fernández-Souto, A. B., & Puentes-Rivera, I. (2015). Las empresas gallegas más contaminantes y su gestión de la comunicación de crisis. In K. Matilla (Ed.), *Casos de Estudio de Relaciones Públicas: Espacios de diálogo e impacto mediático* (pp. 33–57). UOC Ediciones.

Giménez-Rivera, M. J. (2019). *Estudio de los clústers del envase y el embalaje en España* [Doctoral dissertation]. Universitat Politècnica de València.

Martínez-Murcia, S. (2019). *El poder transformador de la industria 4.0: análisis de su influencia en el clúster del automóvil en España* [Doctoral dissertation]. Universitat Politècnica de València].

Miquel-Segarra, S., & Aced-Toledano, C. (2019). Objectives and difficulties in the evaluation of internal communication in Spanish companies. *El profesional de la información, 28*(5). https://doi.org/10.3145/epi.2019.sep.21

Moreno, Á., & Capriotti, P. (2006). La comunicación de las empresas españolas en sus Webs corporativas. Análisis de la información de responsabilidad social, ciudadanía corporativa y desarrollo sostenible. *ZER, 11*(21), 47–62. http://www.ehu.eus/ojs/index.php/Zer/article/view/3718/3348

Peco-Lahuerta, D., Tarragona, M. P., & Scarpellini, S. (2019). *Análisis de fuentes de financiación de empresas integrantes del clúster del porcino en España* [Trabajo Fin de Grado]. Universidad Zaragoza.

PRnoticias (2018). *Informe PR2018*. prnoticias. https://bit.ly/2yVs0zR

Rodríguez-Fernández, L., & Vázquez-Sande, P. (2019). Retos y perspectivas en la comunicación organizacional. *El profesional de la Información, 28*(5). https://doi.org/10.3145/epi.2019.sep.01

Salvador-Peris, P. (1999). Comunicación e imagen en las ONG. *Fòrum de Recerca, 5*(26), 1–12. http://repositori.uji.es/xmlui/bitstream/hand-le/10234/79956/forum_1999_3.pdf?sequence=1&isAllowed=y

Sánchez-García, E. (2021). *Aglomeración industrial, capital social y capacidad de absorción como impulsores del desempeño innovador y empresarial: una aplicación al sector de suministro de energía eléctrica, gas, vapor y aire acondicionado en España* [Doctoral Thesis]. Universidad de Alicante.

Simón Onieva, J. E. (2015). *Gabinetes de comunicación universitarios y redes sociales* [Doctoral Thesis]. Universidad de Almería. https://www.educacion.gob.es/teseo/imprimirFicheroTesis.do?idFichero=pcYLFv9VX0w%3D

Onoris Metz-Galán, Adrián Cordero-Redondo,
Alejandro Álvarez-Nobell, and Ana Bélgica Guichardo-Bretón

The situation of strategic communication and public relations in the Dominican Republic

Abstract: This study seeks to contribute to the efforts being made to characterize the current state of the professional field of public relations (PR) in Central America and the Caribbean. We deal with the reality of the Dominican Republic from initial exploratory research on the studies and associative development it has had; a closed survey of 153 professionals active in the field of strategic communication and PR, media and academia. In addition to the socio-demographic profile of the sample, the importance and contribution to the organization were investigated: functions and areas, leadership and role of Dircom, evaluation strategies, the role of agencies, and aspects such as the ethical dimension. The results showed an incipient development of the profession in the Dominican Republic, especially in strategic and political functions. Strategic planning is not fully developed, and evaluation and measurement are areas of little professionalization. There is also great potential in outsourced services and ethical dilemmas. In general, the results suggest the need for professional associative and specialized postgraduate training in the field of PR in the Dominican Republic. In addition, it highlights the importance of conducting macro-surveys or sectoral studies to obtain a map of the current state of PR in the region, which in turn can have an impact on educational policies, regulatory frameworks, and sectoral improvements. The discipline of PR is a professional and disciplinary field in constant change and with important challenges in relation to current contexts, the environmental crisis, and the transformation of the culture of work and organizations.

Keywords: public relations, strategic communication, Dominican Republic, dircom, macro-surveys

1. Introduction

The importance of corporate communication or public relations as a professional activity in the Dominican Republic has been gradually increasing over the last 20 years. At the same time, the characteristics of the departments of communication have also evolved, growing in budget and structure as well as incorporating new areas of work. Therefore, the figure of Communication Directors (and those who perform the function) has also evolved, gaining greater prominence and functions in the Steering Committees of companies, especially in large ones.

As a result, the Association of Communication Directors of the Dominican Republic (*AsoDircom*) emerged in 2016. This process that has taken place in the country should be understood above all by the profound transformation of a context where the internet, technology, digital ecosystem and social networks have created a new paradigm for the communication of organizations. In addition, the Dominican Republic also receives a great influence from international trends in the Public Relations sector, particularly from the Spanish market. However, this perception and impulse does not have systematic data that allows for the study of the characterization and development of the activity and its prospects.

As in other parts of the world, communication in Dominican organizations has been strongly influenced by journalism and the work of journalists. Nevertheless, more and more public and private entities are focusing on managing communication in a strategic, comprehensive and integrated manner with all their stakeholders.

In 2017, UNESCO carried out a study on media development in the Dominican Republic in which it made evident an x-ray of the structure and, consequently, the influence on other disciplines and professions, such as communication in organizations or public relations that are being articulated. The 203-page study incipiently mentions public relations when it refers to work performed by journalists: “19.2 % work in a government public relations office (…), 7.1 % own their own public relations firm; and 6 % work in a private corporate communication” (Grullón Morillo, 2017, pp. 26 and 27); or when it refers to university training offerings and enrollment levels (pages 27, 172 and 173). On page 156 there is an interesting reference to a certain incompatibility that implies for journalists a “mixed exercise”; fulfilling functions in the media and public relations tasks. This scarcity of data on the sector’s activity is also notorious in a country with a little-studied media history (Cruz Sánchez, 1994).

In response, there are already international (Zerfass et al., 2021) and regional studies of high prestige in the strategic communication and public relations sector, such as the Latin American Communication Monitor (Álvarez-Nobell et al., 2021; Moreno et al., 2015, 2017, 2019) that highlight its relevance and provide systematic data supported by high methodological and theoretical standards. Already in 2012, Molleda et al. warned about the importance of macro-surveys in the profession to know the current development and trends in a comparative and longitudinal way. They also present limitations and risks (Moreno & Humanes, 2009) that demand the need for greater depth and contact with the local reality and context.

However, in regions such as the Caribbean or Central America, there are no national chapters. Along these lines, the International Journal of Public Relations[1]

---

1 https://revistarelacionespublicas.uma.es/index.php/revrrpp/issue/view/23.

recently devoted a monograph to the importance of the discipline in the region (Saladrigas-Medina & Mena-Young, 2021), constituting a very important precedent in this regard. Despite this, data on the Dominican Republic is scarce, which showcases the need for more sectoral studies.

Based on the need for information on the state of communication in the country, which would provide the academy and the industry in the Dominican Republic with evidence on the sector, we set up our project with three main objectives:

1. *To initiate a performative compilation of the most important milestones and antecedents with the purpose of elaborating a historiographic memory of the profession and the sector in the Dominican Republic.*
2. *To form a first general database of current active professionals in the fields of strategic communication and public relations, media and academia.*
3. *Determine and characterize the professional profile (gender, age, profession, seniority, training) and the variables that identify the activity in the Dominican Republic such as: its importance and contribution to the organization; functions and areas; leadership and role of the Dircom; evaluation strategies and tools; activity of the agencies and consultancy; and ethical dilemmas.*

2. Literature review

The first line of work yields these results, which we present in a non-systematic and unfinished way, that constitute the initial theoretical framework of the project. At this stage, we have applied a perspective of the Grounded Theory (Bonilla & López, 2016; Lúquez & Fernández, 2016; Morita et al., 2017). We thus carry out a construction of the theorization based on the description and ordering/classification of possible theoretical categories, all stemming from narratives, actors, and actions related to the phenomenon under study. This proposal arises from the complexity of perspectives that exist in Latin America regarding the role of professionals in organizational communication and public relations (Arzuaga-Williams, 2019; Fallas, 2014; Krohling Kunsch, 2011).

In this sense, the proposal by Athaydes et al. (2022), which "dissects" the methodological strategy for a high-impact academic and professional macrostudy in the continent such as the Latin American Communication Monitor, has also been particularly useful in the proposed design.

In turn, the imprint that academic training leaves on the development of competencies and professional skills in the field of public relations (Álvarez-Flores et al., 2018; Armendáriz, 2015; Gutiérrez-García & Sadi, 2020) justifies a particular effort to analyze the progress that this field has had in the Dominican Republic.

2.1 Public relations in the Dominican Republic: Early precedent

The initial push from the public sector

According to historical data, in 1940, during the Trujillo dictatorship, there was an "information office for journalists." At the same time, on August 18, 1954, the first "Press Department" was created by the Dominican Government where a journalist was hired as an employee, placed at an empty desk, without an office or clear responsibilities. Dr. Rafael Molina Morillo recounts in his work "Mis recuerdos imborrables" (my unforgettable memories), that while he was a reporter for the newspaper El Caribe he met with the dictator Rafael Leonidas Trujillo in Spain, where he was studying and, upon seeing him, he insisted that he must visit him at the Palace once he returned to the country. He narrates how when he arrived at the presidential house to comply with the request of the President of the Dominican Republic, he was informed that by request of "El jefe"—as they used to call him—he had been appointed Press Officer of the Secretary of the Presidency (a position that had not existed until then) with the mission of providing official information to the media (Molina Morillo, 2013). Another of the first public relations offices set up in the public sector was that of the *Banco Agrícola* in 1961.

However, it was in the period between 2008 and 2012 when the central government's headquarters developed for the first time a comprehensive communication strategy with the aim of unifying and grouping the different government sectors in the so-called communication cabinets to manage in a unified way the common problems that affect the different sectors. With the "integral communication strategy," the Communication Directorate of the President's Office initiated training processes for those who were performing the function of communication management in government entities. To this end, courses on hypermedia were offered at the José Martí International Institute of Journalism in Havana, Cuba, as well as summer courses specialized in journalism, radio and television with the support and faculty of the University of Salamanca, as well as crisis management training conducted by the Spanish company *Asesores de Comunicación Pública*. Other activities led by the Presidential Communications Directorate included annual seminars on planning and relationship building (Núñez, 2012).

In the 2012–2016 governmental period, the President of the Republic creates through the Decree 490–12 the General Directorate of Communication (*DICOM*)[2]

2 https://archivo.presidencia.gob.do/dicom.

under the Ministry of the Presidency, responsible for the coordination of the Communication Policies and the function of Spokesperson of the Government, as well as the integration of the Sectorial Cabinets of Communication into a single structure. In addition, it is in charge of appointing the General Directorate of Communication as the governing body of the Government Communication System.

Some of the functions of the General Directorate of Communication mentioned are:

- *Facilitate Government-Society communication.*
- *Formulate, plan, execute and evaluate the communication policies and strategies of the national government.*
- *Manage the Government Communication System (SICOM).*
- *Manage the communicational actions of the President of the Republic.*
- *Empower citizens, businesses and families, of public policies for their benefit.*

On September 29, 2020, Decree Number. 513–20 amends Article 1 of Decree No. 490–12, granting sufficient autonomy to the President's Press Office to allow it to fulfill its attributions in an efficient manner, under the dependence of the Administrative Ministry of the Presidency.

On September 6, 2021, Decree Number. 542–21 is issued, which creates, in its article 6, the Press Office of the President of the Republic, under the Administrative Ministry of the Presidency, in place of the Directorate of Information and Press of the Presidency, with the purpose of managing the communication actions of the President of the Republic.

During this period, the figure of the Director of Communications (*DIRCOM*) became more relevant in public institutions, and the use of this term became more frequent.

Development in the private sector

In the private sector in the Dominican Republic, communication has been developing progressively, especially in the financial sector and multinational companies. In 1950, the company *Astilleros Dominicanos* created an area with the name of "public relations." In 1959, The Shell Company installed the first office in the country to manage the organization's communication. After the fall of the dictatorship a significant growth in public relations took place in the Dominican Republic as foreign investment increased and companies with a longer tradition in the practice of public relations began to arrive in the country. An example is the Dominican Telephone Company (*CODETEL*) that arrived in the country in 1962.

Gradually it takes on the constant changes that occur in this professional field, assuming an active role in the field of social responsibility, corporate governance, crisis management, institutional image, digital communication, among others. Particularly in financial institutions and multinationals with a presence in the country, communication directors are currently at the highest levels of management, becoming a key piece when it comes to decision-making and the success of these companies.

Other companies in the private sector, especially small and medium-sized ones, until recently did not attach much importance to communication with their target audiences, this need has increased in recent years with digital communication and, above all, with the development of social networks.

2.2 Communication in undergraduate and graduate studies: The role of universities

The Autonomous University of Santo Domingo (*UASD*) is the first center of higher education to include in its curricula a Bachelor's Degree in Communication Sciences by means of the Law No. 3476–53 of January 24, 1953, during the Trujillo dictatorship,[3] but it was not until 1994 that the *UASD* offered a study plan of social communication with references to: Journalism, Graphic Arts and Public Relations, thus becoming the first higher education institution to offer a degree in Public Relations.

In September 2020, the School of Communication of the *UASD* announced to the media that after 20 years it would open the second cohort of the master's degree in strategic communication and public relations (Diario Libre, August 13, 2020).

Meanwhile, the Pontificia Universidad Católica Madre y Maestra (PUCMM) as of 2002 included in its academic offering's undergraduate studies in Social Communication, initially at the Santiago campus, while at the Santo Tomás de Aquino Campus, in Santo Domingo, the degree program had its first students in 2003. In 2009, the Academic Council of the PUCMM approved the shift toward a focus on Audiovisual Production and Corporate Communication in the Social Communication degree program. A third curricular reform was carried out in 2016, with a focus on competencies, including in its curricula bachelor's degrees in Audiovisual Communication and Cinematographic Arts and, for the first time, the bachelor's in Corporate Communication.

---

3 T. Vidal Rodríguez, https://elnacional.com.do/escuela-comunicacion-social-uasd-cumple-68-anos/.

In 2005, the *PUCMM* began to offer a new master's degree in corporate communication management at the Santiago campus, a dual degree program with the EAE Business School in Spain, with a faculty made up of Dominican and Spanish professors. It became the first postgraduate studies program in corporate communication in the Dominican Republic, a program that has been to this date taught uninterruptedly.

In 2017 the University *APEC-UNAPEC* unveiled its bachelor's degree in digital communication and more recently, in 2022, presented its new bachelor's degree in communication and Multiplatform Journalism. In terms of postgraduate studies, it has among its programs a master's degree in corporate communication management, offered since 2009.

An element of great importance for the development of Corporate Communication and the figure of the Communication Management in recent years has been how the lack of an attractive offer of postgraduate programs within the country or the seeking of new approaches and experiences has led to many Dominican students pursuing a master's degree in communication to do so in another country, particularly Spain or the United States.

International training has been fundamental for the development of corporate communication in the private sector, given the limited options that existed in the country, it was possible for national professionals to acquire the necessary competencies to achieve the advances that have been experienced.

This allowed, among other multiple advantages, that those who had obtained such knowledge (as well as degrees) once they joined their respective companies and organizations could help shape increasingly specialized and professionalized communication departments from the inside.

2.3 Communication congresses, conferences and awards in the Dominican Republic

One of the initiatives held annually is organized by the Central Bank of the Dominican Republic. These are communication seminars aimed at communication directors of public and private companies, public relations professionals, teachers and students of communication, to learn about advances and share experiences in corporate communication. The seminar has addressed, among other topics, the corporate storytelling, corporate identity, corporate purpose, internal communication and crisis communication.

The School of Communication of the *Pontificia Universidad Católica Madre y Maestra* organized a series of seminars on public relations from 2004 to 2007, which later became corporate communication seminars until 2018. Since 2021, the Corporate Communication Symposium has been held, with the participation of national and international experts. These seminars seek to become a space for the exchange and updating of knowledge on corporate communication with lectures, exchange of best practices, showcasing of successful cases and recognition to students, brands, companies or corporations for their innovative practices.

The "Corporate Communication Day Awards to Outstanding Companies" was created in 2021 by the School of Communication of PUCMM[4] at its Santo Domingo campus, with the goal of promoting good practices in the exercise of the career, as an example of campaigns, positive actions, to bolster more humane and sustainable companies through the impact of communication strategies and management of internal audiences. To ensure transparency in the selection of the award, a nomination process is carried out on the website, in which the public proposes the candidates who are then evaluated by a qualified jury.

2.4 Corporate communications and public relations associations

As mentioned above, in June 2016, the Professional Association of Communication Directors of the Dominican Republic (Asodircom) was created as a non-profit organization that brings together corporate communication and public relations managers of companies and institutions in the Dominican Republic. *Asodircom's* objective is the defense and recognition of the figure, role and functions of communication professionals in companies, institutions, associations and all types of public and private organizations.

During *Asodircom's* time in operation, the entity has entered strategic alliances with *Dircom-España* and other international associations in the field of communication, public relations and reputation. In addition, *Asodircom* has been holding international meetings on different topics of corporate communication with internationally renowned professionals. It has also actively participated in events such as *Cibercom*.

Other corporate communications and public relations associations in the Dominican Republic that have driven a relevant transformation of the sector such as:

- The Association of Communication and Public Relations Companies (*ADECORP*) was incorporated as a non-profit organization in 2013

4 https://www.diariolibre.com/actualidad/nacional/2022/11/18/pucmm-entrega-reconocimientos-en-are-a-de-comunicacion/2145443.

with the purpose of promoting the development and professionalism of communication and public relations services, as well as promoting the use and services of communication as a strategic tool for development. *ADECORP* was born to promote professional training and the development of university and technical programs in public relations and communication, serve as a forum for exchange with other similar national and international organizations, represent its members and establish ethical standards that encourage fair competition in the communication services market. This association is formed by more than 50 national companies and a little more than 10 international agencies operating in the country.

- The Dominican Circle of Public Relations Professionals (*CIDOPREP*), a non-profit organization that brings together professionals who practice this discipline, was founded on May 15, 2001. Subsequently, in October 2017, it became the Dominican Association of Public Relations Professionals (*ASODOPREP*).
- In November 2022, the Dominican Association of Internal Communications (*ADOCI)* was created as an initiative of a group of dynamic and prestigious professionals positioned in the management of this area. *ADOCI* is a collaborative platform, which seeks to motivate the permanent development of new competencies in the professionals of the area, to promote scientific and innovative practices and strengthen the sector in the country. One of the objectives pursued by the association is to generate a conversation around new trends in internal communication, analyze and promote the progress, development and role currently played by the function of Internal Communication in the Dominican Republic, to create spaces for collaborative learning and improve management in organizations and professional updating to develop new practices in the sector.

2.5 The PR and communication consultancy sector

An example of the development experienced by corporate communication in recent years in the Dominican Republic is that the Dominican market, where several agencies were already operating (McCann, Porter Novelli, Pagés BBDO; Ogilvy, Mullenlowe Interamerica, etc.), has broadened to a number of international agencies that have opened offices in the country (LLyC, Newlink, Villafañe & Asociados, Pizzolante, Atrevia, etc.), which has logically allowed the development of projects incorporating the latest trends, products and methodologies that are being implemented in other countries. This has created a favorable context in which services can expand and become more and more competitive.

3. Methodology

The study starts without having an existing database of professionals practicing in the country. The level of development of the associations in this sense is very basic. The review and systematization of background information that we carried out have allowed us to create, in line with the second objective, a current general database of active professionals in the field of strategic communication and public relations, the media and the academic field. This database was prepared by data mining, consulting the different sector actors involved. The original basis has been the list of university graduates. Its verification and formation was carried out during December 2022 and March 2023; 533 contacts were collected via telephone and digital. This is a first precedent in this sense that should grow. The publication and dissemination of these results also seek to make this situation visible and ensure that the initial database grows in the future.

From this first population, a simple random sample of 153 participants was selected. Three emails were sent to the database, trying to achieve a sample that was as diverse as possible in terms of profiles, fields, gender and seniority. Those selected completed a closed online form of 21 questions during February 2023. The form was previously tested by five professionals in the sector.

This empirical work allowed us to obtain relevant and representative information to determine and characterize the professional profile (gender, age, profession, profession, etc.) and the variables that identify the activity in the Dominican Republic, such as its importance and contribution to the organization, the functions and areas, the leadership and role of Dircom, evaluation strategies and tools, agency and consulting activity, dilemmas and consulting, ethical dilemmas and the level of associativism.

The Statistical Package for the Social Sciences (SPSS) was used to analyze the data. The results have been tested to determine their statistical significance depending on the variable (Chi^2, ANOVA / Scheffé Post-hoc-Test, *t*-test of independent samples, Pearson correlation, Kendall rank correlation or Mann-Whitney U Test).

4. Results

We present below the results obtained from the tabulation and analysis of the survey data.

4.1 Demographic profile

The profile of working professionals in Public Relations Communication, according to our study, is made up of 24.8 % men and 75.2 % women. Compared to international studies, there is an average of 50 % more women. In terms of age, 77 % are over 30 years of age, with a significant percentage of professionals over 50 years of age (Figure 1).

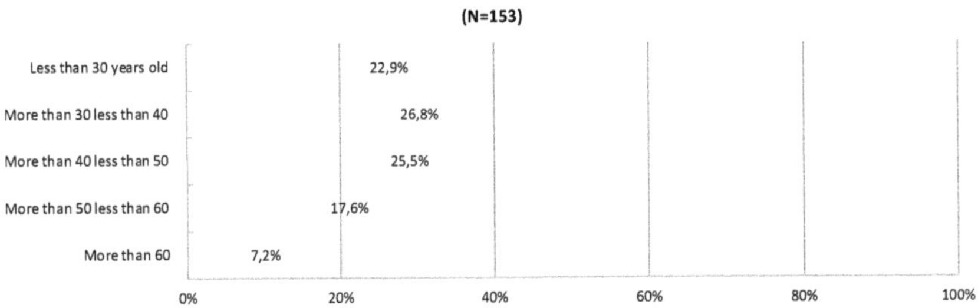

Figure 1. Age of professionals.

Source: authors' own.

Regarding training and education, the level of professionals is very high, with more than 90 % of them having at least a bachelor's degree. In addition, postgraduate training is significantly more extensive than the international average, with almost 75 % of professionals obtaining them (specialty 11.8 %; master's 59.5 %; and doctorate 2 %) (Figure 2).

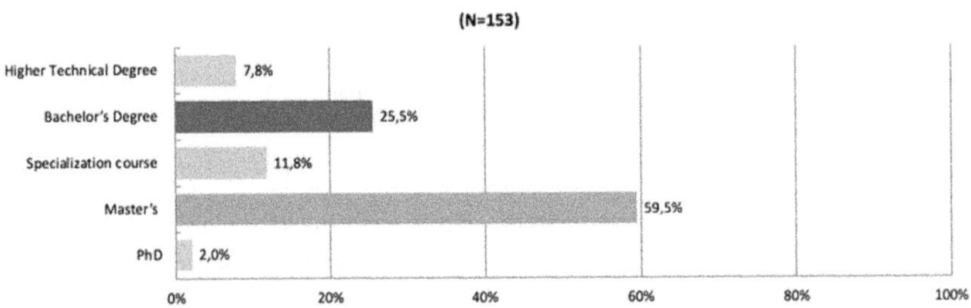

Figure 2. Level of education.

Source: authors' own.

When we inquired about the disciplines of training (between undergraduate and postgraduate), the respondents mostly said that they came from the field of public relations and corporate communication, followed by marketing and advertising, and finally journalism. An interesting fact, which is also studied in other macro-surveys, is the amount of time working in the field. Thirty-two percent have been in the field for less than 10 years; another 32 % between 10 and 19 years; 21 % between 20 and 29 years; and finally, 15 % with more than 30 years.

4.2 Importance and contribution of communication in organizations

The first of the questions we asked about was the current importance of corporate communication in the different types of organizations in the DR (Figure 3). It appears that both in the private sector (large companies) as well as in the public sector, the importance is very high. It is in the third sector, where the valuation (very important) is comparatively lower and does not reach 50 %. In addition, 13.7 % consider it not at all important for NGOs, and 7.2 % for SMEs.

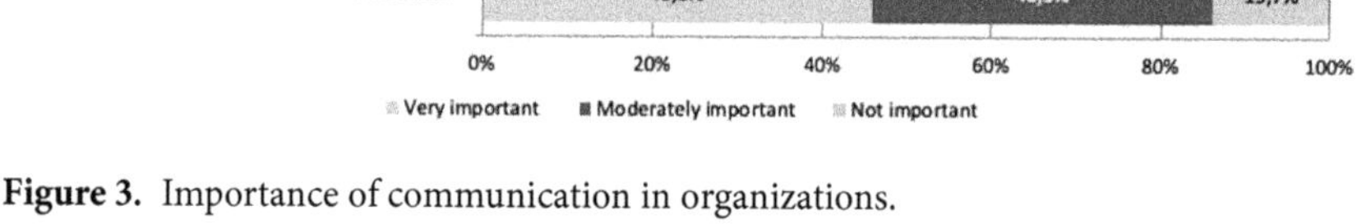

Figure 3. Importance of communication in organizations.
Source: authors' own.

When assessing the contribution of communication in organizations in the DR (Figure 4), 94.8 % stated that it is "key to the adoption of a common purpose and the trust-building" as being; followed by 89.5 % for its "contribution to ensuring security and proactive management of potential conflicts, risks and even crises."

It is very noticeable, given the importance of the issue today, that 5.2 % say that it is "Not at all important" for the company to contribute to the security and proactive management of gender-equality and equity objectives and policies.

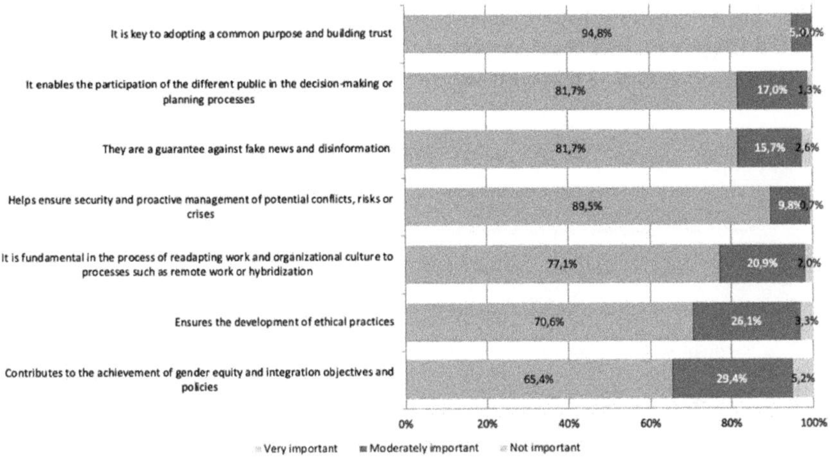

Figure 4. Contribution of communication to organization.

Source: authors' own.

4.3 Functions and management areas

The second block of work on which we inquired has to do with the functions and areas of management carried out in organizations (of all types) in the DR (Figure 5). In this case, 100 % stated that the main function is to plan and direct the strategies that allow for a positive positioning of the organization among the public.

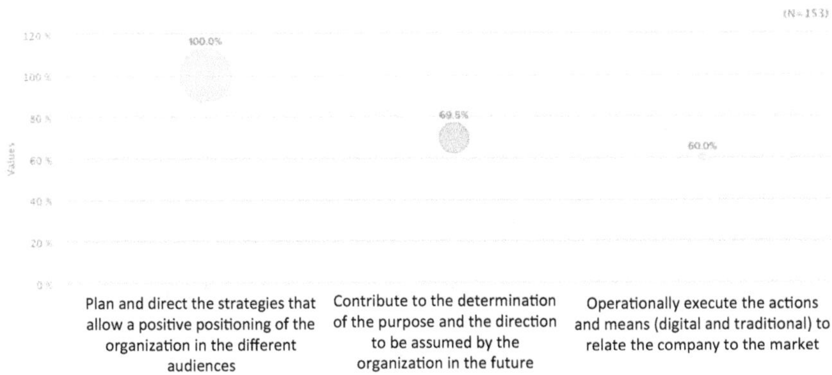

Figure 5. Functions of communication in the organization.

Source: authors' own.

As for the communication departments and/or areas in the organizations in the DR (Figure 6), 79.1 % are concerned with press relations, 74.5 % with digital communication and 55.6 % with events organizations, ceremonial, and protocol.

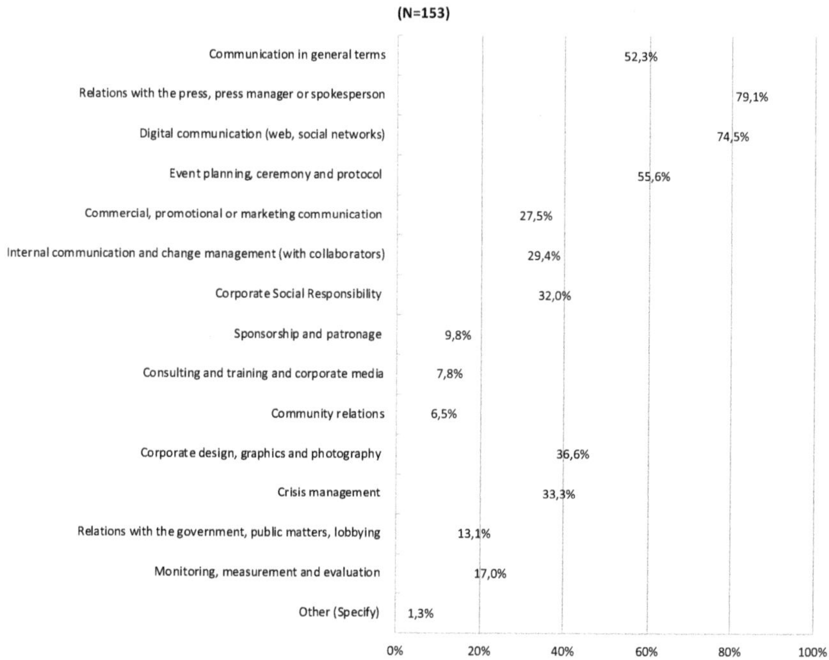

Figure 6. Departments and areas of communication in organizations in the DR.
Source: authors' own.

A key aspect in shaping the public relations function is the analysis of the areas of communication and their importance, but from a prospective perspective (Figure 7). In this case, DR professionals consider that, in 2026, the most important areas will be "communication, sustainability and social responsibility" (66 %); "digital communication" (64.1 %); and "internal communication and change management" (51 %). Close behind, with 49 %, is "crisis management."

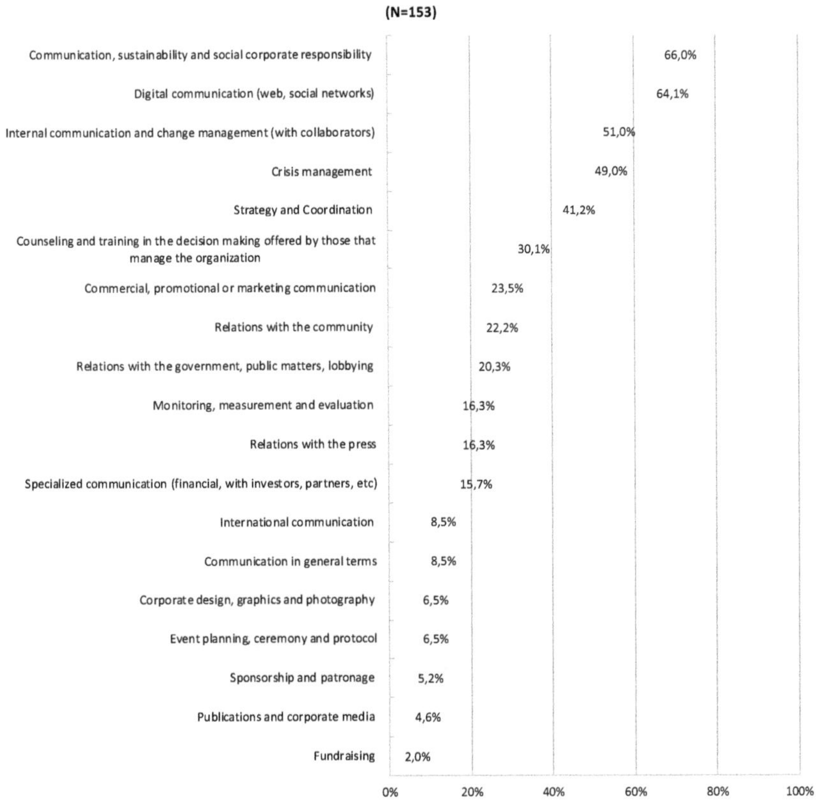

Figure 7. Most important areas in 2026.
Source: authors' own.

4.4 Leadership and role of *Dircom*

The next block addressed the assessment of those who exercise the responsibility for the communication of organizations in the DR (Figure 8), and their involvement (with a permanent and strategic role) in the governing bodies and steering and/or decision-making committees. The data shows that, in the DR, 52.9 % always participate on a permanent and strategic basis. Also, 41.8 % do so in an advisory capacity and have made requests in certain situations. But the most relevant fact is that there are still 5.2 % who do not see any reason for the managerial function of communication.

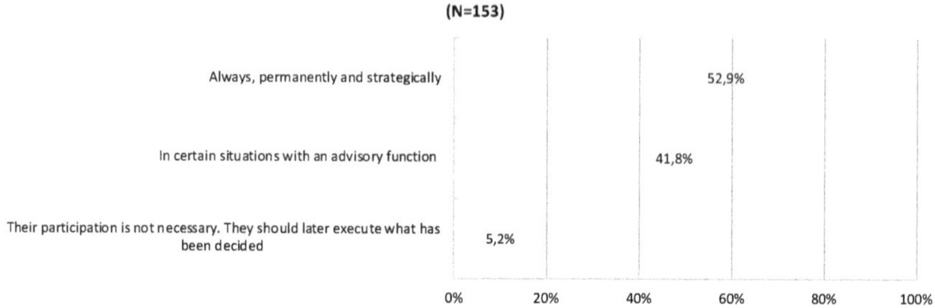

Figure 8. Strategic leadership and advisory function.
Source: authors' own.

When the same question was asked, but in the context of a crisis, a subtle increase (to 62.7 %) can be observed in the participation of the person in charge of communication (*Dircom*) with a permanent and strategic role (with decision-making power) in the crisis committees that manage these exceptional situations in the organizations (Figure 9).

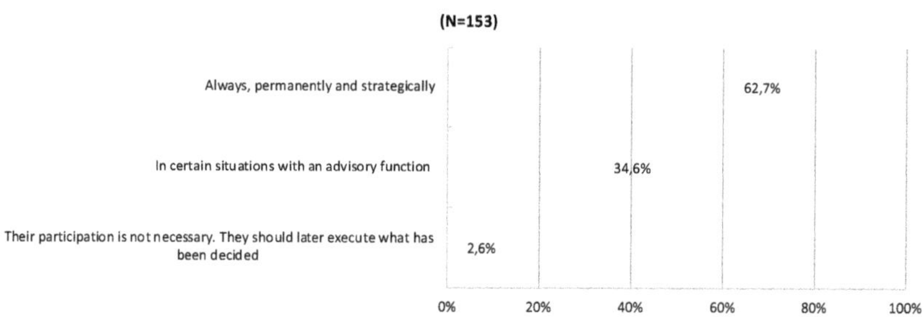

Figure 9. Communication and crises.
Source: authors' own.

4.5 Evaluation strategies

The measurement and evaluation function is one of the stages of communication planning that has been most developed and has had the greatest impact on the legitimacy and development of the activity at the professional level. In this sense, we paid special attention to assess how communication managers (*Dircom*) were believed to be accountable for their management in the DR (Figure 10). In this regard, it can be seen that the lowest levels of impact are the ones that are given most importance: the analysis and reporting of positive impacts in the media (79.1 %) followed by tracking in social networks and digital environments (66.7 %).

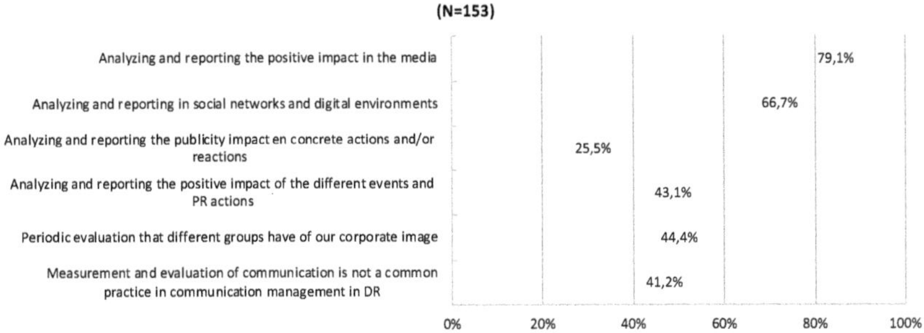

Figure 10. Measurement and evaluation tools.
Source: authors' own.

As for the indicators considered to be the most appropriate for measuring the results of the implementation of communication strategies, in line with the previous answer, metrics of impact on social networks, web audience measurements and ROI in their cost-benefit are the most important and common (Figure 11).

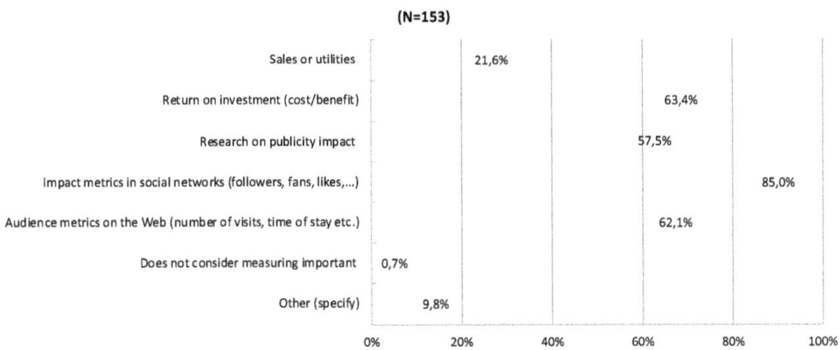

Figure 11. Top-rated measurement and evaluation indicators.
Source: authors' own.

A very interesting aspect is that the study has made it possible to investigate the analysis and identification of audiences and the use of technology for their management (Figure 12). In this regard, Big Data (75.2 %) leads the way.

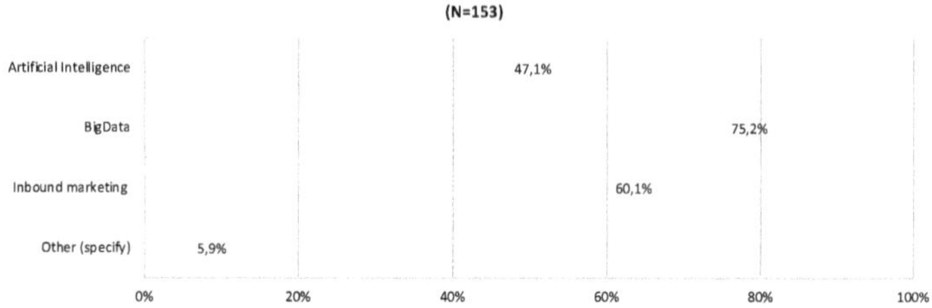

Figure 12. Technological tools known to identify audiences and their needs.
Source: authors' own.

4.6 The role of agencies and consulting

There is no doubt that agencies and consulting are a key dimension of public relations management. In the case of the DR (Figure 13), they mostly take on operational roles such as press, events and digital communication management. More strategic functions are barely covered.

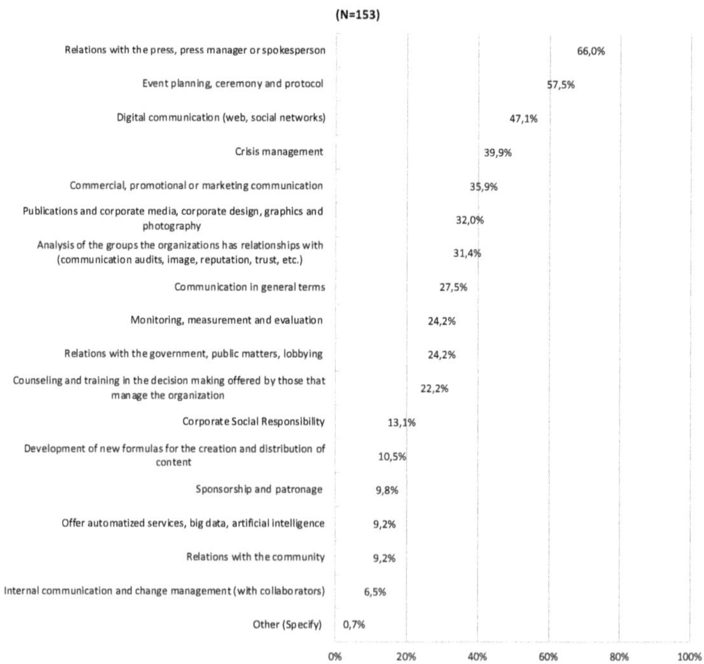

Figure 13. Main functions of external agencies and consulting firms.
Source: authors' own.

4.7 Ethical dimension

Finally, we inquired about this aspect that emerged in the UNESCO report, regarding the ethical dilemma and the alleged absence of conflict of interest when a practicing journalist carrying out his or her professional activity in a communication media also works in PR consulting. The data is complex to understand (Figure 14).

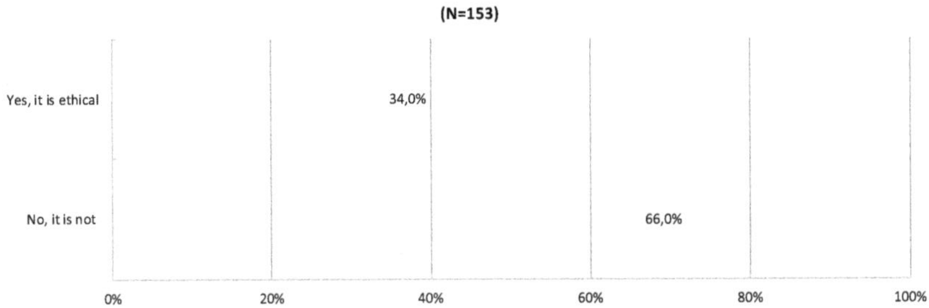

Figure 14. Ethical dimension.
Source: authors' own.

It is notable that the majority (66 %) consider it unethical for practicing journalists to also perform consulting work, which evidently may represent a clear conflict of interest. This situation is largely due to what the Dominican College of Journalists (*CDP*) has repeatedly denounced regarding the fact that journalism is one of the lowest-paid professions in the Dominican Republic. For this reason, many professionals need to work multiple jobs to survive and those who can only get one job have a very hard time, despite working many hours a day, in order to obtain a regular remuneration. This economic limitation is coupled with various complications and occupational hazards that threaten the physical integrity, health and daily journalistic performance.

5. Discussion and conclusion

The results show an initiatory development of the profession, particularly in the strategic and political functions. Innovation is correlated to the development shown by the training, the degree of importance and the assumed contribution of the communication function in organizations.

Strategic planning is not developed in all its phases, and the evaluation and measurement function is an area of little professionalization. The results show a great potential in outsourced services and ethical dilemmas are present among the sector's opinions. Finally, there is a marked need for professional associativism and specialized postgraduate training.

Public relations is a professional and disciplinary field in constant change and with very great challenges in relation to the current contexts, the environmental crisis, and the transformation of work culture and organizations. The macro-surveys or sectoral studies make it possible to observe an x-ray of the current state in a longitudinal and comparative way. At the same time, going deeper into national chapters allows for regional anchoring and systematization of data that should later have an impact on educational policies, regulatory frameworks, and sectoral improvements.

Due to the importance of deontology and ethics in the field of PR, it is evident that the future of the profession in the country also depends on sensitizing entrepreneurs, executives, and media owners to facilitate better conditions for the practice of journalism within an ethical framework.

The collaboration of Dominican associations and universities with international institutions, associations and PR organizations to develop new research, exchange knowledge, learn about best practices and success stories, access new methodologies and learn about new evaluation and measurement systems can help to promote the profession in a more dynamic way while complying with the most current standards.

Based on the findings, a set of challenges and key areas for improvement in the field of public relations in the Dominican Republic are identified.

- *Strategic planning development:* Strengthening this aspect will require training public relations professionals in advanced strategic planning techniques and providing resources to facilitate their implementation across various types of organizations.
- *Professionalization in evaluation and measurement:* Establishing clear standards and effective evaluation methods to measure the impact of public relations activities is crucial. Specific training in this area and the implementation of tracking and analysis technologies could contribute to improving this aspect.
- *Ethics and deontology:* Promoting a strong ethical culture in the practice of public relations is essential. This could be achieved through awareness and education programs emphasizing the importance of integrity and professional responsibility.

- *Professional association and specialized training:* To foster a more robust professional development, it is crucial to promote collaboration between local and international associations and universities. This will facilitate knowledge exchange, adoption of best practices, and access to advanced methodologies and evaluation systems. Moreover, specialized postgraduate training could help elevate the level of professionalism in the field.
- *Adaptation to current contextual changes:* It is critical for public relations professionals to be prepared to adapt and effectively respond to these changes. This may involve continuous training and greater integration of sustainability strategies and corporate social responsibility in public relations practices.

Overall, addressing these challenges requires a comprehensive approach involving educational institutions, as well as stakeholders in the sector, including associations and business organizations. Such studies reflecting the state of communication in the country, with methodological rigor and periodicity, should serve as a starting point.

References

Álvarez-Flores, E. P., Núñez-Gómez, P., & Olivares-Santamarina, J. P. (2018). Perfiles profesionales y salidas laborales para graduados en Publicidad y Relaciones públicas: de la especialización a la hibridación. *El profesional de la información* (EPI), *27*(1), 136–147. https://doi.org/10.3145/epi.2018.ene.13

Álvarez-Nobell, A., Molleda, J. C., Moreno, A., Athaydes, A., Suárez-Monsalve, A. M., & Herrera, M. (2021). *Comunicación estratégica y relaciones públicas en América Latina: crisis del COVID-19 en la gestión de comunicación, ciberseguridad, situación de las mujeres, retos éticos y nuevas competencias.* Resultados de una encuesta en 20 países. EUPRERA.

Armendáriz, E. (2015). El nuevo perfil del profesional de la Comunicación y las Relaciones Públicas. Una visión desde la perspectiva del mercado. *Revista internacional de relaciones públicas*, *5*(9), 153–178. http://dx.doi.org/10.5783/RIRP-9-2015-09-153-178

Arzuaga-Williams, M. (2019). Perspectivas latinoamericanas sobre el rol de los profesionales de la comunicación organizacional y las relaciones públicas. *Anagramas Rumbos y sentidos de la comunicación*, *17*(34), 135–154. https://doi.org/10.22395/angr.v17n34a7

Athaydes, A., Álvarez-Nobell, A., & Molleda, J. (2022). Latin American Communication Monitor: estrategia metodológica para un macroestudio de alto impacto académico y profesional en el continente. In L. Marroquín (Ed.), *Comunicación en Contextos Socioorganizativos, Aportes*

Teórico—Metodológicos (pp. 161–174). CICOM. https://cicom.ucr.ac.cr/wp-content/uploads/2022/11/Comunicacion-En-Contextos-Sociorganizativos-Aportes-Teorico-Metodologicos.pdf?fbclid=IwAR2uz9pTS6prfM9vTuP7FmaHjrAZxta6V4wilZjuNOp3txAxkzWthMwksnU

Bonilla-García, M. Á., & López-Suárez, A. D. (2016). Ejemplificación del proceso metodológico de la teoría fundamentada. *Cinta de moebio, 57*, 305–315. https://doi.org/10.4067/S0717-554X2016000300006

Cruz Sánchez, F. (1994). *Historia de los medios de comunicación en República Dominicana* [Doctoral dissertation]. Universidad Autónoma de Santo Domingo.

Fallas, C. (2014). Central America. In T. Watson (Ed.), *Latin American and Caribbean perspectives on the development of public relations: Other voices* (pp. 45–60). Palgrave MacMillan.

Grullón Morillo, A. (2017). *Análisis del desarrollo mediático en República Dominicana: basado en la aplicación de los indicadores de desarrollo mediático de la UNESCO*. UNESCO Publishing.

Gutiérrez-García, E., & Sadi, G. (2020). Capacidades profesionales para el mañana de la comunicación estratégica: contribuciones desde España y Argentina. *Revista de Comunicación, 19*(1), 125–148. https://doi.org/10.26441/RC19.1-2020-A8

Krohling Kunsch, M. (2011). Comunicação Organizacional e Relações Públicas: Perspectivas dos estudos Latino-Americanos. *Revista Internacional de Relaciones Públicas, 1*(1), 69–96. http://dx.doi.org/10.5783/RIRP-1-2011-03-69-96

Lúquez, P., & Fernández, O. (2016). La teoría fundamentada: precisiones epistemológicas, teórico-conceptuales, metodológicas y aportes a las ciencias. *Cumbres, 2*(1), 101–114.

Molina Morillo, R. (2013). *Mis Recuerdos Imborrables*. Editora Corripio

Moreno, Á., & Humanes, M. L. (2009). Limitaciones y riesgos de la investigación transcultural en Relaciones Públicas y Comunicación estratégica. El auge de las macroencuestas. *Revista Latina de Comunicación Social, 64*, 646–653. https://doi.org/10.4185/10.4185/RLCS-64-2009-851-646-653

Moreno, Á., Molleda, J. C., Álvarez-Nobell, A., Herrera, M., Athaydes, A., & Monsalve, A. M. S. (2019). *Latin American Communication Monitor 2018–2019: Comunicación estratégica y sus retos: Fake new, confianza, Información para la toma de decisiones, liderazgo, satisfacción, estrés y compromiso laboral. Resultados de una encuesta en 19 países*. EUPRERA.

Moreno, Á., Molleda, J. C., Athaydes, A., & Monsalve, A. M. S. (2015). *Latin American Communication Monitor 2014–2015: Excelencia en comunicación estratégica, trabajo en la era digital, social media y profesionalización. Resultados de una encuesta en 18 países*. EUPRERA.

Morita Alexander, A., Escudero Nahón, A., & García Ramírez, T. (2017). Cerrando la brecha de las competencias profesionales genéricas: un estudio de Teoría Fundamentada. *Revista Iberoamericana de Educación*. https://doi.org/10.35362/rie7511354

Nuñez, R. (2012). *Gabinetes de comunicación gubernamental: experiencia dominicana*. República Dominicana.

Saladrigas Medinah, M., & Mena Young, M. (2021). Relaciones Públicas en Centroamérica y el Caribe. *Revista Internacional de Relaciones Públicas, 11*(22), 1–4. http://dx.doi.org/10.5783/RIRP-22-2021-01-01-04

Zerfass, A., Buhmann, A., Tench, R., Verčič, D., & Moreno, A. (2021). *European Communication Monitor 2021. CommTech and digital infrastructure, video-conferencing, and future roles for communication professionals. Results of a survey in 46 countries*. EUPRERA/EACD.

María Isabel Míguez González, Juan Manuel Corbacho Valencia, and Jesús Pérez Seoane

The evolution of public relations trends over the last five years according to the most relevant professional reports in the sector

Abstract: Like any other relevant economic sector, the public relations sector must adapt to changes, especially those triggered by COVID-19. It is important to understand the trends that have marked the pandemic, its changes and consolidations. For this purpose, a qualitative analysis is carried out, both nationally and internationally, of the annual reports of the most representative professional associations in the sector, such as DIRCOM, EUPRERA, USC Center for Public Relations and Corporate Excellence Center for Reputation Leadership. With the aim of detecting the incidence of the pandemic, the five-year period covering the two years prior to the outbreak of COVID-19 up to the present day. The main results show a coincidence in highlighting the phenomenon of post-truth and the spread of fake news (and with it the key role of public relations in the fight against it), purpose, the need to generate trust, leadership, ethics, transparency, sustainability, technological advances, digitalization and cybersecurity. In any case, the latest editions of the reports show positive and encouraging data for the future of the PR industry.

Keywords: trends, public relations, DIRCOM, EUPRERA, USC Center for Public Relations, Corporate Excellence Center for Reputation Leadership

1. Introduction

Changes in the media, technology, society and the structures and mechanisms themselves for managing organizations means communication and public relations experts must evolve and constantly adapt to new trends. It is crucial they are aware of these trends since this will help them gain an insight into the needs and demands of the public, anticipate changes and adapt to them, identify opportunities for innovation, improve communication in organizations and be up-to-date in terms of the latest tools and technologies so as to work more efficiently.

For this reason, different institutions and associations strive to create periodical reports which identify, almost in real time, and even anticipate the most important issues institutions and those industry professionals should be concerned with. On carrying out a diachronic analysis of these documents trends over time can be observed as well as its consolidation over time. This helps to determine whether they are fleeting whims or important issues that will eventually become fundamental to exercising the profession.

Moreover, COVID-19 has had an important impact on corporate communication. Seeing the need to have new ways of communicating with employees, customers and other interest groups, the pace adoption of new technologies and communication tools has increased. With so many employees working at home and facing uncertainty, the role of internal communication has become crucial for keeping them informed, motivated, and committed. Therefore, companies have had to adapt the way they carry out internal communication in order to reach them more effectively, using digital tools such as participative platforms and video conferences. They have also had to strive to reach consumers more effectively who are in an increasingly saturated digital environment and satisfy other interest groups whose demand for information has risen.

With this in mind, the aim of this study is to analyze some of the most important reports in the sector over a five-year period, including the two years before the outbreak of COVID-19 and the two after it. Thus, the following objectives were set:

1. To analyze the main focal points of the different reports in a particular way.
2. To identify the similarities and differences in the trends detected in different reports and contexts.
3. To evaluate the impact the pandemic has had on communication trends and how the identified trends have evolved, how they might continue and how important they are.

2. Theoretical framework

Although in the academic world much effort has been put into reflecting the most important trends and changes in communications and public relations, the different reports drawn up by professional associations in the sector are what have painted this reality most accurately and brought it up to date, especially those which are published on an annual basis.

One of the most active associations in this respect in Spain is the Association of Communication Directives (Dircom). Created in 1992, in 1996 it published the first edition of *Anuario de la comunicación* (Communication Yearbook). This is a publication that, for 26 years, has continuously collated the main trends and reflections from experts by means of reports, round tables, news and interviews. Thus, Dircom has become a living memory of how the profession has evolved in Spain. Dircom also carries out another leading study, the report *El Estado de la Comunicación en España/The State of Communication in Spain* (Dircom, 2022), which comes out on an irregular basis. The data from this report provides an insight into professional reality focusing on aspects such as the functions of communication departments and employee profiles. In recent years, Dircom has also created other interesting research such as *Informe Inclucom/Inclucom Report* (Dircom, 2019), which analyzes inclusion and skills for professional development for people with a disability who work in the field of communication in Spain. Apart from that, *Informe Gendercom/Gendercom Report* (Dircom, 2018) focuses on the breaches in and opportunities for enhancing gender-equality in the communication field in Spain.

Apart from publications by Dircom, also worth mentioning in Spain is the work carried out by Corporate Excellence—Center for Reputation Leadership, a corporate foundation created in 2011 from a merger of the Foro de Reputación Corporativa/Forum for Corporate Reputation (2002) and the Instituto de Análisis de los Intangibles/Institute of Analysis of Intangibles (2004), whose aim is to drive professionalization and manage key intangibles in companies. Reputation, brand, corporate communication and public affairs are some of the issues they focus on. However, they also have a knowledge ecosystem with many documents that members may consult. One of the most important contributions in terms of analyzing trends is the *Approaching the Future* report drawn up in partnership with Canvas Estrategias Sostenibles, whose first edition came out in 2016, 20 years after the first *Anuario de la Comunicación* came out and with a very different professional outlook. This report is specifically aimed at detecting trends related to reputation and managing intangibles.

Extending the focus to Europe, also worth mentioning as a leading entity is the *European Public Relations Education and Research Association* (EUPRERA). Although the association adopted this name in the year 2000, it was originally called the CERP Education & Research, founded in France in 1959. With almost 500 members from 40 countries (not all of which are in Europe), the association carries out numerous activities aimed at advancing research and knowledge about communicative strategy and public relations in the continent. As for analyzing trends, its main contribution is the *European Communication Monitor* (ECM), which has been annually implemented since 2007 by partners from different universities, spearheaded and organized by EUPRERA in partnership with the *European Association of Communication Directors* (EACD). Based on surveys conducted throughout Europe and spread freely on the Internet, this report shows the professional reality of communication experts and managers, as well as their employment conditions and salaries. They also delve into strategic matters these experts must face and focus on different aspects in each issue. Since 2015, EUPRERA has also published the *Latin American Communication Monitor*, focused on Spanish and Portuguese-speaking countries. However, this study only comes out every two years.

If we broaden the focus from a geographical point of view, also worth mentioning is *Global Communication Report* drawn up by the USC Center for Public Relations. The importance of this report, from the University of Southern California, lies in the fact it is made with the participation of many public relations entities, among which are the Institute for Public Relations, the Global Alliance for Public Relations and Communication Management, the PR council and the PRSA. First published in 2017, the *Global Communication Report* is a look at the profession within an American context. However, it also provides valuable reflections for the profession as a whole and anticipates trends whose effects transcend North America. In fact, its methodology is based on an online survey for public relations students and experts out of which almost a half (the percentage varies slightly depending on the year) are not American.

All this research has been cited frequently by academics and researchers from the field of public relations. Also, different studies mention the reports drawn up by Dircom (Almansa & Fernández-Souto, 2020; Costa-Sánchez et al., 2020a, 2020b, 2020c; Rodríguez-Fernández & Vázquez-Sande, 2019) and Corporate Excellence (Ruiz-Mora et al., 2022), adding the trends they have indicated to the academic research.

For ECM, the authors themselves make use of the valuable data supplied by the monitor to carry out an academic analysis of its different aspects (Tench, 2020; Verhoeven et al., 2018). Other researchers from different countries such as Spain (Acuña, 2018; Castillo-Esparica & Villabona-Beltrán, 2018; Costa-Sánchez et al., 2020a, 2020c; Cuenca-Fontbona et al., 2020; Rodríguez-Fernández & Vázquez-Sande, 2019) and Portugal (Sebastião, 2022; Sebastião & Spínola, 2021) have also used ECM data in their studies.

Lastly, although the Global Communication Report is a far cry from the specific circumstances of public relations in Spain, certain Spanish academics (Costa et al., 2019; Mendieta-Ramírez & Estrada-Rodríguez, 2022; Rodríguez-Fernández & Vázquez-Sande, 2019) have appreciated its findings.

4. Methods

To address the subject matter of this study the content analysis has been used in a qualitative manner. A five-year period was chosen for this study and which covered the two previous years and the two ones after the pandemic. A sampling procedure was deemed to be the most appropriate, and the editions from 2018 to 2022 of four significant reports from different geographical areas (international, European and Spanish) were chosen for analysis, as well as annual periodicity as additional selection criteria. As a result, the sample was made up of the following documents: Global Communication Report (USC Annenberg Center for Public Relations, 2018, 2019, 2020, 2021, 2022), European Communication Monitor (promoted by EUPRERA and EACD) (Zerfass et al., 2018, 2019, 2020, 2021, 2022), *Approaching the Future* (Corporate Excellence and CANVAS Estrategias Sostenibles, 2018, 2019, 2020, 2021, 2022) and Anuario de la Comunicación (Dircom, 2018a, 2019a, 2020, 2021, 2022a).

For the analysis, firstly an inductive identification of trends was carried out from reading the different reports. Next, the diachronic trends collected in each report were plotted. Lastly, the different trends identified were reorganized and grouped in order to set a common comparative framework that could be applied to all reports and for extracting common patterns.

5. Results

5.1 Anuario Dircom

The 2018 Anuario Dircom, under the generic title *La era de los bots con inteligencia emocional* (*The Era of Bots with Emotional Intelligence*) shows the potential artificial intelligence has. However, it also reveals, for example, how little AI is implemented in daily corporate life with bots. It covers the role of reputation and trust in a post-truth and disinformation era, and alludes to the significance of corporate purpose, emphatic listening and the role Dircom has as a custodian of the cultural values of the organization. It also highlights the significant role visual communication has due to its great potential and effectiveness. From a managerial point of view, it explores the Dircom profile and its skills and stresses the strategic relationship there needs to be between marketing and comunicación, although it indicates that in this symbiosis the functions of communicative management must be well defined.

The 2019 annuary entitled *La transformación del Dircom, capacidad de evolución* (*The Dircom Transformation, Capacity to Evolve*) mentions the first trend as being ethics and truth, highlighting the demand for hyper transparency, the search for authenticity and the importance of value-based messages. It also addresses the potential blockchain technology has when applied to communication, although its implementation is still in its fledgling years. In the chapter on communication and people it takes an in-depth look at the significance of a work-family balance and a good work environment as requirements professionals have when choosing a company. The growth in brands with purpose and the ongoing problem of measuring intangibles are other two key trends the report mentions.

In the year 2020, the Annuary inaugurated its open digital format and under the title *Impulsando un futuro más sostenible* (*Driving a More Sustainable Future*), analyzed sustainability and the green economy as an opportunity for companies to seize. The chapter dedicated to people looks at the importance of listening, internal communication and leadership. As for technology, there is an exploration of the changes this has brought to the labor market, and it looks at the role of artificial intelligence and chatbots and the revolution in home working. Moreover, it indicates the need to humanize technology by means of emotional intelligence.

Big data and cybersecurity (technology used for communication) are the core themes in the 2021 Anuario Dircom. They dedicate their platforms and chapters to these topics, although they are organized according to classical concepts such as external communication, internal communication, social networks and other platforms, crisis communication, and ethics and communication. The push for digitalization and its influence on public relations and communicative processes, the value of data management and the importance of the human factor for making the correct interpretation, the new opportunities to detect threats to reputation and the need to check data and sources are the salient issues in this edition.

Lastly, the 2022 Anuario Dircom, entitled *Comunicación para una nueva sociedad/Communication for a new Society* praises the figure of Dircom and is organized around three large topics. The first is technology and innovation which tests how adaptable Dircom is, with elements such as the metaverse or the web 3.0. The second concerns culture, which must be consistent in businesses, people are deemed to be the greatest corporate asset, and when companies are socially committed they will find it easier to attract talent. Finally, the last issue is sustainability in which Dircom is seen as the broadcaster of environmental, social and governance commitments (ESG) endorsed by organizations.

5.2 Approaching the future

The *Approaching the Future* report organizes its contents around four large blocks and stresses the fields which the Corporate Excellence—Center for Reputation Leadership focuses on per se. Therefore, firstly, it includes a block that highlights the main trends, under the name global trends, transversal trends and macrotrends. Next, a section on reputation is included which since 2019 has become "reputation and brand." The third block is for sustainability, and the last one was called "ethics and corporate governance" in 2018 and from 2019 onward became "ethics and transparency." The transversal trends collected in the first block may be considered to be the most significant in the year and many will be interrelated, as well as to the other blocks in the report. In any event, and regardless of the block dealt with, the topical trends which the *Approaching the Future* report focuses on have not varied greatly in the period studied.

Therefore, in the 2018 report the first global trend shown was the fall in trust, and purpose was mentioned as a catalyst for helping recovery and its importance within the sustainability block was studied. By 2019 purpose was considered to be a transversal trend, the most significant that year according to experts, and has remained like that until the last report came out in which purpose was already an established managerial model for organizations.

The contextual elements related to post-truth and uncertainty, understood as being conditioning factors for communicative activity, were also analyzed as a transversal trend closely link to politics in 2018 and 2019. Uncertainty remained among the trends in 2020 and 2021 when the pandemic and its results were the main topics.

Another omnipresent topic in the report is digitalization, stated as a macrotrend in all reports apart from in 2020, although that year too there was talk of technology, transparency and the data privacy dilemma with artificial intelligence.

Other transversal trends identified by the report were diversity (2018), the climate emergency (2020 and 2021) and leadership (2021 and 2022). In all reports ESG criteria or socially responsible investment, and sustainable development goals and the 2030 agenda were also mentioned, albeit not as the main trends.

5.3 European communication monitor

This report fundamentally focuses on matters related to exercising communication and the conditions in which it is practiced. Although it covers different aspects every year, there are three elements that remain constant in all the reports analyzed: strategic matters for communication, salaries, and the features of excellent communication departments. Apart from these, each report focuses on some specific elements which are reflected in the title of the report itself.

Therefore, in 2018, the ECM deals with strategic communication and the challenges posed by the rise of fake news. It also covers issues concerning trust and leadership and provides data on the work stress suffered by communication experts and the slight fall in work satisfaction vis-à-vis previous reports.

In 2019 confidence in the profession and the way in which transparency is managed becomes the key element. Also, the professionals are asked about the incorporation of artificial intelligence and the new content strategies organizations use.

The 2020 report explores the ethical challenges in the profession and stresses the need for professional training in this area. It also addressed gender-equality, and demonstrated the endurance of gender prejudices and the glass ceiling. Apart from that it looks at problems for cybersecurity in organizations and explores the professional skills used in strategic communication.

In 2021 the use of communication technologies and digital infrastructures are analyzed by professionals, demonstrating that companies are far more advanced in this respect than are tertiary sector institutions and organizations. The use of video calls and future roles of communication professionals are analyzed specifically.

Lastly, in 2022 the monitor considers diversity, equality and inclusion as challenges for the profession and the trend in emphatic leadership is explored. Once again it tackles the use of communication and digital transformation technologies and explores trends in external communication consultancies.

5.4 Global communication report

Every year this report has a core theme determined by its title, although in the contents different aspects may be explored.

In the year 2018, the main theme is how ethics has evolved and this is covered in a professional context. It must be stressed that in this report changes in the industry driven by new technologies and the evolution of the media, the expansion of services provided by public relations consultancies, and the multiplication of professional skills needed in this field are heralded. There is also a need to reinforce an ethical approach in order to have a positive effect on society and attract new talent.

The 2019 report is also largely aimed at professional practice. Here the focus is on technology applied to communication. It warns that with technology there is a higher risk of disinformation and of polarizing the general public. However, it also marks an important driving force for the industry and entails sweeping changes to it.

In the year 2020 the report turns to more contextualized matters and once again explores the activism pervading society. It mentions an activism in which young people participate with whom communicators must learn to work. This is because these new groups, made up of ordinary people, will become more influential in the future and will drive change. Although COVID-19 is mentioned in the report, there is no in-depth exploration of its effects on the communication industry.

The 2021 report is dedicated to politics, polarization and purpose. Although reflections on the role of politics in the creation of a divided and polarized society are largely confined to an American context, the conclusions on the need to have purposeful communication which helps to find solutions to problems and strengthen the values of organizations, can be applied universally.

Lastly, the 2022 report goes back to activism as the main topic although this time it looks at corporate activism. The text considers how the social polarization of public relations work and how social problems such as promoting diversity and inclusion can be tackled from a business perspective. The potential purpose has is stressed as a key element for long-term corporate success as is the role companies have as activists for topics such as climate change.

5.5 Comparative analysis of the most outstanding trends

The detailed analysis of the reports enabled a series of trends to be detected which are repeated with greater or less frequency, according to the field, and establishes a diachronic line for its trend, the results of this analysis are summarized in Table 1, where it can be seen to what extent each report addresses the indicated topic: a clearer tone reflects a tangible treatment of the topic while darker tones show the most significant topics in each report in the corresponding year.

	2018				2019				2020				2021				2022			
	AD	ATF	ECM	GCR	AD	ATF	ECM	GCR	AD	ATF	ECM	GCR	AD	ATF	ECM	GCR	AD	ATF	ECM	GCR
Polarisation																				
Uncertainty/crisis																				
Post-truth and fake news																				
Culture and talent																				
Diversity, equality and inclusion																				
Purpose																				
Reputation and brand																				
Trust																				
Leadership																				
Activism																				
Ethics																				
Transparency																				
Sustainability																				
Climate Change																				
Technology																				
Digitalization																				
Cybersecurity																				
AI and Big data.																				
Communication strategy																				
Professional/profession																				

Table 1. Main trends covered by the reports analyzed
Source: authors' own.

6. Discussion and conclusions

This research shows the general concern over certain contextual elements which directly affect the communication industry. Since 2018 the post-truth phenomena and the extension of fake news (associated with social polarization and uncertainty) which is the subject of the analysis of the reports from the sector both nationally and internationally. Although the uncertainty referred to concerns the first years with the political situation, in 2020 with the pandemic means it is extended to a broader social context and even reaches the very foundations of the industry. This trend is also reflected in the academic literature of the discipline with a great deal of studies that cover the practice of public relations during the pandemic. They reflect on the role of communication experts in times of crisis (Castillo et al., 2020; Xifra, 2020) and explore the phenomena of fake news (Gomes Gonçalves et al., 2022). However, perhaps the most significant conclusion is the year 2022 is the first in which the reports appear to be more optimistic and leave the worries of previous years behind. This reflects the industry is adapting to the new post-pandemic reality or *new normal*.

Despite the pandemic, some trends that were already strong in 2018 continued and were consolidated in this five-year period. Therefore, focusing on the trend seen in *Approaching the Future* and *Global Communication Report*, purpose becomes the main way of managing intangibles in businesses and is linked to corporate activism. Although corporate purpose issues have been researched, particularly from a business perspective, some Spanish academics specializing in public relations have also included this as an interesting element in their research (Pallarés-Renau et al., 2022). Moreover, it is likely that it will become significant as an academic subject, as companies use it more in forthcoming years.

Moreover, the need to build trust, especially within the context of uncertainty described previously and the significance of leadership has remained constant during this five-year period as important elements for building reputation, a concept that is still crucial. For these aspects in particular, a monograph is dedicated to Doxa Comunicación for 2020 coordinated from the public relations field (Carretón-Ballester & Viñarás-Abad, 2020). Therefore, even though one may think of increased trust and leadership as a result of the pandemic, the truth is these two aspects were already contemplated in reports before the outbreak of COVID-19.

However, the driving force in the industry, according to different reports, is technological progress and digitalization. The potential big data and artificial intelligence has and the use of new media and technology-linked support are the main elements referred to in some 2018 reports and remain constant in the following years. This is in keeping with the academic focus on these aspects; Pereira-Villazón et al. (2019) identified a total of 41 academic articles in 2017 which covered big data in public relations and Cuenca-Fontbona et al. (2020) concluded that 75 % of communication and public relations agencies in Spain were at an advanced stage in their digital transformation. This trend was clearly driven, as shown in the reports analyzed, by COVID-19, which led to an increase in the use of technologies in different contexts and has made online communication with internal and external audiences more necessary than ever.

The rise of technology comes hand in hand with concern over cybersecurity, which is reflected by the European Communication Monitor (2020), Anuario de la communication (2021) and the *Approaching the Future* report (2022). This was of equal interest to the Latin American Communication Monitor (2020–2021), which does not include the analysis as it is a study that is carried out every two years, but is also a significant reference for identifying trends. No doubt, cybersecurity and the implications it will have for communication will be ever more important in the future.

Another area that has aroused ever more interest, especially in national studies, is sustainability and particularly, climate change, which the *Approaching the Future* report echoes systematically throughout the period analyzed and Anuario Dircom covers it in the 2020 and 2022 editions. This is largely related to its adoption by the UN General Assembly for the 2030 Agenda and the objectives for sustainable development. Interest in this is reflected in different studies from a public relations perspective (Álvarez-Nobell et al., 2020; Barroso et al., 2023; Estanyol, 2020). Therefore, there is a patent need for companies to integrate the standards marked by the 2030 agenda into their managerial strategy, and reflect them in their purpose. This reinforces the role communication has as a mechanism for transferring the new values organizations endorse to their audiences and society in general

Sustainability encompasses both ethics and transparency, two topics that all reports, at one time, focus on and are mentioned in the study by Almansa and Fernández-Souto (2020) on the trends and challenges posed for public relations experts. Also cited in this study is the significance of equality and inclusion, which along with diversity, are explored especially in the *Approaching the Future* report and in the ECM, which is of special interest in terms of gender; in this respect, a positive trend is detected in a corporate setting, although there is still some way to go and fully integrating people is a great challenge for the twenty-first century.

Lastly, all reports analyze in detail the function of communication and the features of professionals or departments, and mention the significance of aspects such as coherence between the communicative and general strategy of organizations, innovation and the capacity to experiment with new means of communication and that of evaluating and measuring the impact of communicative activities. In this respect, no substantial variations were observed throughout a five-year period and the difficulties detected, such as, for evaluating and stressing intangibles, are still among the concerns experts have.

In short, the outbreak of the pandemic, which, at first, seemed to shatter the social order in different ways, has left its mark on the communicative industry in terms of digitalization and the use of different channels and supports. However, the fundamental trends seen in previous years have not changed. Indeed, they have been reinforced and consolidated.

Acknowledgments

This study is supported by the SEPCOM research group (Universidade de Vigo).

References

Acuña, B. P. (2018). Revision and prospective of visuality in the European Communication Monitor 2017. *CUICIID, 2018*(1), 329. https://bit.ly/3XMJmZ4

Almansa-Martínez, A., & Fernández-Souto, A. B. (2020). Professional public relations (PR) trends and challenges. *El Profesional de la Información, 29*(3). https://doi.org/10.3145/epi.2020.may.03

Álvarez-Nobell, A., Barroso, M. B., & Ruiz-Mora, I. (2020). Propósito, sostenibilidad y conversaciones en empresas de triple impacto. Los ODS en la comunicación digital en las B Corps# BestForTheWorld2019. In T. Hidalgo Marí, F. J. Herrero Gutiérrez, & J. Segarra-Saavedra (Eds.), *Comunicación, periodismo y sociedad: retos profesionales en tiempos de crisis* (pp. 127–149). Fragua.

Barroso, M. B., Castillo-Esparcia, A., & Ruiz-Mora, I. (2023). La dimensión medioambiental y los ODS en la comunicación estratégica de las empresas de triple impacto. *Estudios sobre el Mensaje Periodístico, 29*(1), 27–42. https://dx.doi.org/10.5209/esmp.80708

Carretón Ballester, M. C., & Viñarás Abad, M. (2020). Las relaciones públicas estratégicas para generar confianza y reputación [presentación del monográfico]. *Doxa Comunicación. Revista Interdisciplinar De Estudios De Comunicación Y Ciencias Sociales, 30*, 179–185. https://bit.ly/3LH6Ed5

Castillo-Esparcia, A., & Villabona-Beltrán, D. (2018). Evaluación para demostrar la efectividad en comunicación y relaciones públicas. Una mirada a las prácticas profesionales desde los Communication Monitor. *Communication Papers, 7*(15), 137–137. https://doi.org/10.33115/udg_bib/cp.v7i15.22188

Castillo-Esparcia, A., Moreno, Á., & Capriotti, P. (2020). Relaciones públicas y comunicación institucional ante la crisis del COVID-19. *Revista Internacional de Relaciones Públicas, 10*(19), 1–6. http://dx.doi.org/10.5783/RIRP-19-2020-01-01-06

Corporate Excellence & CANVAS Estrategias Sostenibles. (2018). *Approaching the future 2018. Tendencias en reputación y gestión de intangibles.* https://bit.ly/45Jskgr

Corporate Excellence & CANVAS Estrategias Sostenibles. (2019). *Approaching the future 2019. Tendencias en reputación y gestión de intangibles.* https://bit.ly/3ZafKSz

Corporate Excellence & CANVAS Estrategias Sostenibles. (2020). *Approaching the future 2020. Tendencias en reputación y gestión de intangibles*. https://bit.ly/3LKsOv2

Corporate Excellence & CANVAS Estrategias Sostenibles. (2021). *Approaching the future 2021. Tendencias en reputación y gestión de intangibles*. https://bit.ly/3ngapMx

Corporate Excellence & CANVAS Estrategias Sostenibles. (2022). *Approaching the future 2022. Tendencias en reputación y gestión de intangibles*. https://bit.ly/3LFiLY5

Costa-Sánchez, C., Túñez-López, M., & Míguez-González, M. I. (2019). Agencias de comunicación en España en la encrucijada digital. Prácticas, perspectivas y visión de futuro. *El Profesional de la Información*, *28*(6). https://doi.org/10.3145/epi.2019.nov.06

Costa-Sánchez, C., Túñez-López, J. M., & Míguez-González, M. I. (2020a). Análise comparativa da gestão da comunicação corporativa em empresas e instituições: o caso da Galiza. *Comunicação e Sociedade*, *2020*, 37–51. https://doi.org/10.17231/comsoc.0(2020).2739

Costa-Sánchez, C., Túñez-López, J. M., & Míguez-González, M. I. (2020b). Gestión de la comunicación en la Pequeña y Mediana Empresa: potencial estratégico, filosofía y tendencia. *Estudios sobre el Mensaje Periodístico*, *26*(3), 927–938. https://doi.org/10.5209/esmp.66244

Costa-Sánchez, C., Túñez-López, J. M., & Miguez-González, M. I. (2020c). Public Relations from a Spanish peripheral region: Normal is not normative. *Public Relations Inquiry*, *10*(2), 197–219. https://doi.org/10.1177/2046147X20979290

Cuenca-Fontbona, J., Matilla, K., & Compte-Pujol, M. (2020). Transformación digital de las agencias de Relaciones Públicas y Comunicación españolas. *El Profesional de la Información*, *29*(3). https://doi.org/10.3145/epi.2020.may.10

Dircom. (2018a). *Anuario de la comunicación 2018. La era de los bots con inteligencia emocional.*

Dircom. (2018b). *Informe Gendercom. Brechas y oportunidades de género en la profesión de gestión de la comunicación en España*. https://bit.ly/42xoTaR

Dircom. (2019a). *Anuario de la comunicación 2019. La transformación del Dircom, capacidad de evolución.*

Dircom. (2019b). *Informe Inclucom. Análisis de la inclusión y capacidades de desarrollo profesional de las personas con discapacidad en el ámbito de la comunicación en España*. https://www.dircom.org/wp-content/uploads/2021/04/Informe-Inclucom.pdf

Dircom. (2020). *Anuario de la comunicación 2020. Impulsando un futuro más sostenible.* https://anuario2020.dircom.org/

Dircom. (2021). *Anuario de la comunicación 2021. Big data y ciberseguridad, tecnología al servicio de la comunicación.* https://anuario2021.dircom.org/

Dircom. (2022a). *Anuario de la comunicación 2022. Comunicación para una nueva sociedad.* https://anuario2022.dircom.org/

Dircom. (2022b). *El Estado de la Comunicación En España (ECE 21–22).* https://www.dircom.org/wp-content/uploads/2022/05/ECE_21-22.pdf

Estanyol, E. (2020). Comunicación de la responsabilidad social corporativa (RSC): Análisis de las campañas más premiadas en 2018. *El Profesional de la Información, 29*(3), e290334. https://doi.org/10.3145/epi.2020.may.34

Gomes Gonçalves, S., Jiménez-Marín, G., & Pulido Polo, M. (2022). Relaciones públicas y fake news en la comunicación corporativa. Una revisión de la literatura / Public relations and fake news in the corporate communication. A literature review. *Revista Internacional De Relaciones Públicas, 12*(23), 93–116. https://bit.ly/4eBhnBH

Mendieta-Ramírez, A., & Estrada-Rodríguez, J. L. (2022). Comunicación política y gestión de crisis ante la pandemia del covid-19. *Revista Iberoamericana de las Ciencias Sociales y Humanísticas: RICSH, 11*(22), 103–119. https://doi.org/10.23913/ricsh.v11i22.291

Pallarés-Renau, M., López-Font, L., & Miquel-Segarra, S. (2022). Misión, Visión y Valores. Elementos determinantes en la construcción de un propósito diferenciador para las organizaciones del Tercer Sector/Mission, Vision and Values. Determining elements in the construction of a differentiating purpose for Third Sector. *Revista Internacional De Relaciones Públicas, 12*(23), 51–72. https://bit.ly/3VOcZqG

Pereira Villazón, T., Portilla Manjón, I., & Rodríguez Salcedo, N. (2019). Big data y Relaciones Públicas: Una revisión bibliográfica del estado de la cuestión. *Revista de comunicación, 18*(1), 151–165. https://doi.org/10.26441/RC18.1-2019-A8

Rodríguez-Fernández, L., & Vázquez-Sande, P. (2019). Retos y perspectivas en la comunicación organizacional. *El Profesional de la Información, 28*(5). https://doi.org/10.3145/epi.2019.sep.01

Ruiz-Mora, I., Guerrero-Navarro, D., & Álvarez-Nobell, A. (2022). Encuentros entre la formación y la profesión de relaciones públicas en Andalucía: Análisis de los estudios universitarios de grado. *VISUAL REVIEW. International Visual Culture Review/Revista Internacional de Cultura Visual, 9*(Monográfico), 1–13. https://doi.org/10.37467/revvisual.v9.3747

Sebastião, S. P. (2022). A adoção e perceção de uso de videoconferência na comunicação com os públicos, em Portugal: resultados do European Communication Monitor 2021. *Estudos em Comunicação, 35*. https://bit.ly/3FK2nBD

Sebastião, S., & Spínola, S.C. (2021). Perceções sobre a provedoria de informação aos decisores e as funções de comunicação estratégica em Portugal: resultados do European Communication Monitor 2018. *Observatorio (OBS*), 15*(1). https://doi.org/10.15847/obsOBS15120211567

Tench, R. (2020). Women in public relations: A thematic analysis of ECM data (2009–2019). In *Women in PR history*. Routledge.

USC Annenberg Center for Public Relations. (2018). *Global Communication Report 2018. The revolution of ethics*. https://bit.ly/3K2Up9A

USC Annenberg Center for Public Relations. (2019). *Global Communication Report 2019. PR Tech: The future of technology in communication*. http://assets.uscannenberg.org/docs/2019-global-communications-report.pdf

USC Annenberg Center for Public Relations. (2020). *Global Communication Report 2020. New activism*. https://bit.ly/3LMvcBy

USC Annenberg Center for Public Relations. (2021). *Global Communication Report 2021. Politics, polarization & purpose*. https://bit.ly/3yWxUN8

USC Annenberg Center for Public Relations. (2022). *Global Communication Report 2022. The future of corporate activism*. https://bit.ly/3LJEgqA

Verhoeven, P., Zerfass, A., Verčič, D., Tench, R., & Moreno, A. (2018). Public relations and the rise of hypermodern values: Exploring the profession in Europe. *Public Relations Review, 44*(4), 471–480. https://doi.org/10.1016/j.pubrev.2018.06.001

Xifra, J. (2020). Comunicación corporativa, relaciones públicas y gestión del riesgo reputacional en tiempos del Covid-19. *El profesional de la información, 29*(2). https://doi.org/10.3145/epi.2020.mar.20

Zerfass, A., Buhmann, A., Tench, R., Verčič, D., & Moreno, A. (2021). *European Communication Monitor 2021. CommTech and digital infrastructure, video-conferencing, and future roles for communication professionals. Results of a survey in 46 countries*. EUPRERA/EACD

Zerfass, A., Moreno, A., Tench, R., Verčič, D., & Buhmann, A. (2022). *European Communication Monitor 2022. Exploring diversity and empathic leadership, CommTech and consulting in communications. Results of a survey in 43 countries*. EUPRERA/EACD.

Zerfass, A., Tench, R., Verhoeven, P., Verčič, D., & Moreno, A. (2018). *European Communication Monitor 2018. Strategic communication and the challenges of fake news, trust, leadership, work stress and job satisfaction. Results of a survey in 48 countries*. EACD/EUPRERA, Quadriga Media Berlin.

Zerfass, A., Verčič, D., Verhoeven, P., Moreno, A., & Tench, R. (2019). *European Communication Monitor 2019. Exploring trust in the profession, transparency, artificial intelligence and new content strategies. Results of a survey in 46 countries*. EUPRERA/EACD.

Zerfass, A., Verhoeven, P., Moreno, A., Tench, R., & Verčič, D. (2020). *European Communication Monitor 2020. Ethical challenges, gender issues, cyber security, and competence gaps in strategic communication. Results of a survey in 44 countries*. EUPRERA/EACD.

www.ingramcontent.com/pod-product-compliance
Ingram Content Group UK Ltd.
Pitfield, Milton Keynes, MK11 3LW, UK
UKHW021014120926
8556IPUK00040B/1139

9 783631 907764